Killer Kids

10 Cases of Kids Who Killed Their Parents

Jonny Cassidy

CONTENTS

Chapter Four:

Chapter Six:

Introduction

Murder has been an unfortunate part of the human experience since time immemorial. In the time we have lived on this planet, people have killed and been killed for virtually every reason you can imagine. Sometimes, the reason is not the focus of investigations and public discourse surrounding these incidents. This usually happens when cases are cut and dry. However, there are cases where the reasons and motives of the killers can become the focal point and change everything.

The questions of reason and motive often come up in family violence incidents, especially those involving children murdering their parents. To most people, something as fundamentally wrong as killing one's parents is unfathomable. Yet despite how far removed from our cultural, social, and legal norms it is, parent murder has happened many times in history. Incidents like these have produced some of the most controversial and infamous murder cases in recent memory.

Murder is always shocking to our sensibilities, but in-family murder tends to stick out and is particularly disconcerting to think about. Murders in the criminal underworld, for instance, are certainly shocking, but they are perceived as something that can be expected and, most importantly, something that's distant from us and doesn't really concern most regular people. When family members kill each other, though, different kinds of questions will pop up as people struggle to grasp how and why such extreme violence could happen in a home, a supposed place of love and sanctuary.

These cases usually take on a special degree of infamy when they happen in peaceful or even affluent communities. These incidents collectively affect people's sense of security, and they threaten the very image that we have of what we consider to be normal family life. Worse yet, because these gruesome crimes have occurred within homes, they are something that comes from within the community, where most of us think we are safe.

At any rate, children have shown throughout history that they are more than capable of murder even against their own parents. Children from all walks of life have carried out these killings for a wide range of reasons, including mental illness, self-defense, revenge, greed, or as a result of arguments that got too heated. Whatever the motives, these cases always carry enormous pain and trauma for those involved and the wider community.

Murder, in general, is a complex enough phenomenon, but how a child becomes a killer, especially of their own parents, is an even deeper question. It is an important question, but it's also one that cannot be answered definitively. Each case has to be looked at individually and completely separate from others, with all its intricacies and context taken into careful consideration. This is precisely what this book will do with ten select cases where children have killed their parents in the most gruesome ways imaginable. These are stories of pain, love, hatred, insanity, and above all, tragedy, all unique in their details but all interwoven with the homicidal potential that continues to lurk in mankind.

CHAPTER ONE:

Jasmine Richardson

Jasmine Richardson was only twelve when she and her 23-year-old boyfriend, Jeremy Allan Steinke, murdered Jasmine's entire family with a knife. This shocking triple murder shook Canada to its core in 2006, leading to a lot of controversy and discussion, particularly regarding the motive. Particularly disturbing was just how seemingly normal the Richardson family was, as well as the fact that the murderous duo also killed Jasmine's 8-year-old brother.

One notable characteristic of the crime scene was an inordinate amount of blood, which even shocked some of the investigators. Referring to the murders as "a major bloodletting event," some of the investigators who had worked on the case noted the extraordinary cruelty and excess violence they encountered at the Richardson home.

Also described as a crime of passion by some because of the romantic dimension the crime had, the Richardson family murders garnered a massive amount of attention. Some viewed the killings as an example of what can happen when young, impressionable girls are manipulated. Others theorized that Oliver Stone's Natural Born Killers was to blame for corrupting the youth, while others also ascribed the case to plain old evil. Seeing as Jasmine's accomplice at one point claimed to be a "300-year-old werewolf," one could be forgiven for suspecting insanity as a factor as well, although this was ruled out in the legal proceedings. Now a free woman since May 2016, Jasmine Richardson was the youngest offender in the history of Canada to be found guilty of more than one first-degree murder.

The Richardson Family and One Problematic Phase

There was hardly anything out of the ordinary about the Richardson family. The parents, Marc and Debra Richardson were 42 and 48 at the time of the murders. Apart from Jasmine, they also had an 8-year-old by the name of Tyler Jacob. By all accounts, they were a loving family that got along well. The Richardson's had relocated to Medicine Hat, Alberta, around three years prior to the crime, and it wasn't long until they acquired a very positive reputation in the neighborhood.

According to one of their neighbors, Bob Grodin, many folks saw the Richardson's as a model family they all aspired to build. Nonetheless, Marc and Debra's lives weren't without turbulence, at least in the past. Both had issues with substance abuse before they met each other and built their new life together. It was in a recovery support group where the couple first met, and they helped each other through their addictions. Between their recovery and their death at the hands of their daughter, Marc and Debra had fifteen years of marriage.

As Jasmine approached twelve years of age, some changes in her behavior and personality gradually became more visible. Initially, changes in behavior, interests, clothing and makeup were easily attributable to the onset of teenage years and the usual behavioral changes at this point in life. Over time, Jasmine seemed to be developing an interest in all things dark. From makeup to clothes to music, Jasmine entered a Goth phase.

When Jasmine started getting in trouble at her Catholic school, there were indications that it might be more than just a phase. Going against the dress code, displaying satanic imagery, and drawing problematic symbols on her skin with ink were only some of the reasons why Jasmine often got reprimanded. Her appearance and behavior also drove other kids away from her, and she soon found herself being avoided. The speed at which these changes occurred is best illustrated by testimonies from some of her friends who described her as kind, gentle, welcoming, friendly, empathetic, and outgoing.

Prior to the onset of these changes in 2005, Jasmine was known as a model student, both in regard to conduct and schoolwork. Now, she was often talking back, disobeying her teachers, cursing, and being overall rebellious. This wayward phase could have been interpreted simply as a natural instance of a young, growing person asserting their personality and identity if only things didn't deteriorate further.

A significant escalation in Jasmine's slide to the dark side came in January 2006 when she met Jeremy Steinke for the first time. According to Jeremy, this match made in hell happened at a punk rock concert, and he immediately left a strong, lasting impression on Jasmine. She had already been immersed in the Goth, punk, and similar subcultures both in real life and on internet forums and social networks, but these fascinations were magnified tenfold by Jeremy.

It wasn't long before Jeremy and Jasmine were dating. Jasmine would routinely sneak out to meet up with her boyfriend, or she would lie to her parents about where she was going, often securing a pass by telling them she was going to study with a friend. This wasn't always possible, so an important part of their relationship was communicating over the Internet.

After getting involved with Jeremy, Jasmine's social media pages started featuring a growing number of ominous signs. Apart from often lying that she was fifteen,

Jasmine would express interest in some very dark subjects and listing notorious serial killer and cannibal Jeffrey Dahmer as one of her heroes was one example. It's certainly not unbecoming of a near-teenager to post immature and stupid things online or to project an edgy image for shock value, but Jasmine soon came to a point where other kids were afraid of her.

The Goth couple's unseemly relationship met immediate disapproval even from Jasmine's friends, who shared her interests and lived a similar lifestyle. One reason for disapproval was the striking age disparity, of course, but Jeremy also had a history of violence and a reputation that left a lot to be desired. Naturally, when Jasmine's parents found out about this relationship, they were appalled not just because of their daughter's youth but also because Jeremy wasn't really an influence that most parents would want around their preteen daughter. Marc and Debra immediately cut off this relationship, grounded their daughter, and forbade her from ever seeing Jeremy again.

This enraged both of them, especially Jeremy, who reportedly blogged about it in early April 2006, going on a tirade against Jasmine's parents, expressing a desire to slit their throats. Jasmine and Jeremy continued to communicate over the Internet, especially through communities and websites they were both registered on, such as VampireFreaks and Nexopia.

Jeremy Steinke and the Massacre

Whereas Jasmine was raised in a loving family environment, Jeremy grew up rough. His father was out of the picture since the boy was a toddler. He lived with his alcoholic mother and her numerous partners, who were often abusive men. Talking about his stepfather, Jeremy said that he abused him and his siblings in various physical and mental ways. Sometimes, the stepfather would tie the kids up and make them watch as he abused one of the other siblings.

Jeremy wasn't given a break in school either, as other kids bullied him, and he always had trouble fitting in. Jeremy lived in very poor conditions, for which he was picked on, often called *Stinky* by bullies. These experiences made him depressed and suicidal, leading him to make attempts on his life before he met Jasmine. Already in his early teens, Jeremy became a strange kid, in a way creating an entirely new identity for himself.

Apart from claiming to be an ancient werewolf, Jeremy added all sorts of peculiarities to his style, such as bizarre jewelry, makeup, and other things that helped him assert his personality. For instance, some acquaintances testified that Jeremy used to wear a vial of blood around his neck. This wasn't the only account of Jeremy's early fascination with blood, as there were also testimonies that he liked the taste of it.

Already by the time he was fifteen, Jeremy was abusing alcohol and engaging in self-harm. Even before he met Jasmine, he had already made a habit of hanging around girls of her age. Jeremy often associated with underage girls at the local mall, perhaps because he found it easier to impress them than the girls of his own age. With a driver's license, his edgy Goth makeup, and an aura of mystery, many young and impressionable girls were drawn to him, especially those who were into the Goth scene, like Jasmine.

Despite Jeremy's online threats and clear motive to murder the Richardson's, subsequent police reports show that it was indeed Jasmine who first floated the idea of killing her parents in an email. Not only did she instigate the crime, but she presented a plan, explicitly stating that she would kill them so she could live with Jeremy. Steinke didn't protest and instead offered his own input on what they should do and how. In fact, even some of Jasmine's friends later testified that she told them she was planning to kill her parents, but these threats were interpreted as jokes.

On the day of the murders, a few hours before the fact, Jeremy watched *Natural Born Killers* with his friends. The movie's plot was strikingly similar to what he and his underage girlfriend were planning to do. Jeremy commented that he was hoping they could do something like that, only without leaving Jasmine's brother alive.

Jeremy would refer to the Oliver Stone flick yet again in his eventual conversations with the police. He called the movie the best love story of all time, enamored by the tale of a young couple who kill the girlfriend's parents and run away together.

On the night of April 22-23 of 2006, Jeremy and Jasmine would make this fantasy a reality, or at least try to. Before the murders, Jeremy drank a sizeable mixture of alcoholic beverages, including beer, vodka, and wine. On top of this, he also took cocaine and ecstasy. Jeremy later talked about how he drank alcohol and took the drugs just before driving over to Jasmine's neighborhood and that he was "off like a rocket."

Armed with a butcher knife, Steinke dressed all in black for this occasion while also wearing a mask. When he arrived at the Richardson residence, he quietly snuck into the home while Jasmine's parents were asleep. However, Debra soon awoke upon hearing noises, and she went downstairs to investigate the commotion. When she found and confronted Jeremy, the attack began immediately, with Jeremy stabbing her multiple times.

Debra's screams as she was being stabbed to death immediately woke up Marc, who rushed downstairs to see what's going on. Hearing clearly that his wife was being attacked, Marc grabbed the nearest item as a weapon, a screwdriver. Marc attacked the killer ferociously in a desperate attempt to defend his family, to which Jeremy later testified. He described that he was caught off guard by this sudden reaction and by how fast Marc made his way downstairs. According to Jeremy, Marc managed to pin Jeremy down to the ground in the struggle, attempting to stab him with the screwdriver while also shoving his thumbs in his eyes.

Steinke eventually managed to overpower his victim and, as he stabbed Marc Richardson to death, he was asked why he was doing any of this. Jeremy answered that this was what Marc's daughter wanted, making this most likely the last thing Marc heard in his life. Jeremy's knife was later found to have a bent tip, indicating that it had hit bone, as Jeremy had stabbed his victim a total of 24 times.

After Jeremy killed the Richardson couple, he and Jasmine met in her 8-year-old brother's room. Jacob had most likely been awoken by the grizzly commotion in the rest of the house. Jasmine found him hiding in his bed, and she most likely stayed with him while Jeremy was killing the rest of the family. After very little consideration, the couple decided that they should kill Jacob as well, based on Jasmine's rationale that he was too young and too sensitive to go on living without his parents. Jasmine first tried to smother her little brother with a pillow while telling him to sleep. After this attempt failed, Jasmine stabbed the little boy five times, mostly in the neck and chest, after which the boy's throat was slit as well.

Apprehension and Aftermath

The gruesome crime started coming to light the very next day. The first person to find the corpses of the Richardson family was a 6-year-old neighbor and friend of Jacob's. He came over to the house hoping to play with his friend, as he did many times prior to that. After receiving no answer to his knocking, the boy took a peek through the window right next to the front door and saw the horrific sight of the massacred bodies of Debra and Marc. He rushed back home to tell his parents what he saw, and they called the police.

The police were quick to respond, and the first to arrive on the scene around 1 p.m. was Brent Secondiak. He first looked through the window and could see at least one body in a very bloody murder scene. He immediately called for backup, and additional detectives and officers soon arrived. The cops then forced their way into the house and started inspecting the crime scene, discovering a nightmarish scene that was sure to haunt them for the rest of their days.

Upon discovering the bodies, the investigators initially had no idea what they were looking at, so they searched the premises for evidence. When they discovered the slain 8-year-old, the police started suspecting the killings were perpetrated by someone close to the family. Once they found a family photograph, which included Jasmine, they realized that the Richardsons' 12-year-old daughter was missing. However, the investigators had no idea that Jasmine had anything to do with the murders, instead suspecting she had been kidnapped. As such, the police's first order of business was to put out an amber alert and start looking for the girl.

The search brought the police to Jasmine's school locker, where they began to find ominous signs. The first clue that there was something wrong with Jasmine was a drawing the police found in the locker, depicting a series of events portrayed with stick figures. The drawing was clearly an illustration of a couple setting a house on fire before running away together, and it was the clue that got the police to start suspecting that Jasmine may not have been a victim. The real shocks came when the investigators started looking into Jasmine's digital trail, particularly her emails and messages with Jeremy.

The runaway couple was tracked down within 24 hours in a town called Leader, some 100 miles away from Medicine Hat, and they were promptly arrested. The arresting officers later testified that both Jeremy and

Jasmine seemed indifferent toward their arrested and their horrific crimes, coming across as carefree and even happy with themselves. Days later, the police also arrested Kacy Lancaster, Jeremy's 19-year-old friend, on the suspicion that she was an accessory to murder since she helped drive the couple and destroy evidence.

According to Canada's Youth Criminal Justice Act, underage minors have certain protection. Jasmine's identity was kept hidden, and she was referred to as "J.R." As circumstances would have it, twelve was the youngest age at which a person could be charged with any crime, and so Jasmine, just like Jeremy, was charged with three counts of first-degree murder. However, for child perpetrators between the ages of twelve and fourteen, the maximum possible sentence was ten years in prison. Jasmine and her defense pleaded not guilty to all charges, saying that her correspondence with Jeremy and others was just hypothetical and that she never really intended to go through with it. However, she told the police that her motive was her love for Jeremy. As she explained, she felt that killing her family would bring the two closer together.

Both killers were found guilty as charged, and Jasmine's verdict was reached on July 9 of 2007, with the maximum ten-year sentence. Apart from prison time, Jasmine also had to go through extensive psychiatric observation programs.

Jeremy's case took a bit longer to reach its epilogue, with the verdict being passed down on December 15 of 2008. For each of the three murders, Jeremy Steinke was given a sentence of life in prison, although he may become eligible for parole after 25 years served. During the legal proceedings, Steinke proposed to Jasmine, to which she agreed, although the marriage never has and probably never will come to fruition.

Jasmine's sentence really did entail a whole lot of rehabilitation, which seemed to have produced considerable results in time. According to the experts who worked on Jasmine's case, she showed great remorse in time and eventually came to accept and regret the full extent of her heinous misdeeds. Her psychiatric evaluations determined that Jasmine possibly had certain personality disorders at the time of the crime, and great efforts were made to rehabilitate and reintegrate her. On May 6, 2016, not long after the anniversary of the Richardson family massacre, Jasmine's rehabilitation program officially ended, and she was released back into the world.

CHAPTER TWO:

Alex and Derek King

O ur first case illustrating that significantly younger children are also capable of deadly violence is the killing of Terry King. Terry was brutally bludgeoned to death by his two sons, Alex and Derek, who were only twelve and thirteen during the heinous act that they committed on November 26, 2001. The killers' youth and the brutality of the murder stand out in this case. It can be difficult or even impossible to determine beyond a reasonable doubt how two young boys got to a point where they would beat their father to death with a baseball bat and then set the house on fire.

The boys' inconsistent, constantly evolving accounts that they gave during the trial made the case even more confusing. The involvement of Ricky Chavis, Terry King's friend, and the abuse that the boys may or may not have experienced at the hands of their father are only some of the factors that complicate the case. This case of patricide is characterized by the fact that both perpetrators have since served their time in prison and been released. This opportunity to create a semblance of normal life after all the bloody ordeals is a rare occurrence that seldom happens in these cases.

Murder, Arson, and the Early Investigation

The killing of Terry King was a particularly gruesome and ferocious affair. The brutal nature of the killings and the age of the perpetrators led many to believe that this must have been a case of abused children taking revenge or trying to defend themselves. As was shown during the trial, however, the case was far from being so clear-cut.

The drama began to unfold on November 26, 2001, when the local firefighters in Escambia County, Florida, rushed to respond to an ongoing fire in the town of Cantonment. The report came in at 1:39 a.m., and by the time the firefighters arrived, the fire was yet to engulf the entire home. In fact, it was in the part of the house that wasn't burning where the firefighters found Terry King's body lying on a couch. Even the first responders on the scene could rule out most fire-related causes for this death since Terry was found with his head severely bashed in.

The subsequent autopsy quickly confirmed that Terry King had died due to blunt force trauma to the head prior to the fire. It was determined that he had been beaten repeatedly and severely with a blunt object, later confirmed to be an aluminum baseball bat. Terry's skull was cracked open, and the heavy blows disfigured a significant portion of his face. Other signs of foul play at the crime scene were the traces of spilled fuel found around the house, clearly indicating that the perpetrators had lit the fire in an attempt to conceal evidence.

Upon questioning the neighbors, Detective John Sanderson and other investigators soon confirmed that Terry King had two sons, both of whom were missing. The very next day, on November 27, both Alex and Derek were brought to the Escambia County Sheriff's Office by Rick Chavis. Rick Chavis was a family acquaintance whose name would keep returning and eventually become one of the key pieces of the murderous puzzle. When Chavis brought the boys in, they turned themselves in to the police, and questioning began. Alex and Derek were interviewed separately by the police, and they were both quick to confess that they indeed murdered their father.

According to their initial statements and confessions, Alex was the one who got the idea to kill Terry while Derek did the work. The murder also featured a degree of premeditation. Derek patiently waited in the evening for his father to doze off on the couch before attacking. In the proceedings following their arrest, the King boys would give conflicting and seemingly ever-changing accounts of many aspects of the case, especially their motives for the murder. They explained that they were afraid of their father and decided to kill him because they feared that he would punish them for running away from home.

Prior to the murder, Alex and Derek spent some time at Rick Chavis' house, even though Terry forbade this in early November. This was despite the fact that Chavis had been a friend of Terry's for several years, pointing to the fact that Terry was growing increasingly uncomfortable with the relationship between his sons and Rick in the time leading up to his death.

However, despite the boys' expression of fear as the cause of the murder, they had to admit that their father never physically abused them. They made mention of being pushed a few times or, at worst, rarely spanked, but they explained most of the supposed abuse as being psychological. According to some of their initial statements, Terry would sometimes stare the boys down menacingly when they did something wrong. On top of that, both Alex and Derek described their father as strict, at least by their standards. The description of these things as "mentally abusive" was given by the boys themselves.

Both Derek and Alex would eventually change their testimonies several times in regard to numerous aspects of the case, not just the responsibility for the murder itself. Most notably, however, the first time the boys decided to change their original statements was when they implicated Chavis in the killing, saying that while they did kill Terry, it was Chavis who talked them into it. Eventually, they changed their story yet again, accusing Chavis of killing their father and then forcing them to take the blame. These accusations would eventually be thrown out, but that would be the least of this case's twists and turns, particularly when it came to Rick Chavis.

On November 28, both Derek and Alex were charged with an open count of murder as the prosecutors prepared their case. Being only thirteen and twelve, Derek and Alex were kept in custody in the Juvenile Detention Center. Despite the abuse allegations that the boys leveled against their father, there was significant difficulty in establishing a clear motive for the crime, which would make the legal proceedings even more controversial than they already were.

Apart from the fact that Derek and Alex were among the youngest individuals in Florida's history to be charged with murder, those observing the trial were also shocked by the disturbing testimonies that came from these troubled youths. Everything from Derek's description of how his father gurgled as he died to the unsettling revelations concerning Rick Chavis shook the nation to its core. Nonetheless, the judge soon decided to try the boys as adults, as allowed by the state of Florida, and a grand jury indicted them both on charges of first-degree murder on December 11 of 2001.

Further Revelations and Rick Chavis

The possible role of Rick Chavis, as well as his general relationship with the King family, had piqued Detective Sanderson's interest right from the start. Before the investigators got to interview Chavis, he received accounts from friends of Terry about his relationship with the boys. It didn't take long for Sanderson to get the sense that something was quite wrong with Chavis.

In the years of friendship between Rick and Terry, Rick had become very close to Derek and Alex. They were so close, in fact, that Rick Chavis was added to the list of people who could pick the boys up from school. The boys would also often spend time at Rick's house, which they much preferred to their dad's home. According to the brothers' testimonies, Terry was strict in the sense that he enforced discipline and rules on them.

On the other hand, Chavis would let them watch TV as much as they wanted to, play video games, and even smoke marijuana. Ten days before Terry's murder, the boys ran away to Chavis' house. After they searched Chavis' phone, the police found a recorded message in which Alex told Chavis that he would like him to tell his dad that neither he nor his brother would ever come back home. In his testimony, Chavis expressed sympathy for these sentiments and corroborated the boys' account of alleged mental abuse while also giving his personal opinion that Terry King was too controlling as a father.

Chavis was also prepared to testify that Terry was abusive if the investigation determined that the brothers were involved in the killing. Besides, he had already voiced his belief that they may have been guilty, as he was aware of the deteriorating relationship between Terry and his sons. Chavis also testified that both Alex and Derek had voiced a wish that their father would die on prior occasions.

Apart from letting minors smoke marijuana at his house, Chavis had various other skeletons in his closet. Most notably, he was a convicted child molester, and, as the investigation and the legal proceedings went on, it came to light that Chavis most likely harbored a sort of sexual obsession with Alex. The sexual dimension brought a lot of added complexity and further blurred the lines in the case. The sexual relationship, which Alex confirmed in his testimony, suddenly created a possible motive for Chavis to kill Terry to prevent him from finding out.

Holes in Chavis's story soon emerged, first in regard to his presence at the crime scene. In the early morning after the fire at Terry's house was put out, James Walker, the step-grandfather of the two King boys, told Detective Sanderson that he had already discussed the events with Chavis. According to Walker, Chavis was the one who told him about the fire while also telling him that Derek and Alex had run away from home. He also said that he entered the house and saw Terry's corpse.

This account was different from the one Chavis would give to Detective Sanderson and his investigative team. During Chavis's first interview, he said that he tried to enter the house but wasn't allowed by the firefighters. More importantly, Chavis told Sanderson that he dropped the King brothers off at home the day before the murder and that he hadn't seen them afterward. Not long after the first interview, the police searched Chavis's home, and details of his relationship with Alex began to emerge.

Strangely enough, the police conducted the search after asking for permission to do so, and they easily found important clues. For one, Chavis kept a picture of Alex right above his bed. Second and more incriminating was the discovery of Alex's personal journal in the attic. In it, Alex had written down quite a few things about his romantic feelings for Chavis. Alex also made reference to a perceived change in his own sexuality, noting that he used to be heterosexual before meeting Rick but that he was now gay.

These findings prompted the investigators to look more closely into Chavis's background. Perhaps unsurprisingly, it was quickly determined that Chavis had a criminal record, which included charges relating to lewd and indecent conduct with young boys in 1984. These charges landed Chavis in prison for six months, plus five years' probation, which was violated in 1986 after Chavis was arrested for burglary and petty theft. He was found guilty and had to serve an additional three years.

The first charges brought up against Chavis relating to the murder of Terry King had him accused of being an accessory to murder. The police accused him not just of giving a hiding place to Alex and Derek following the murder of Terry but also of actively helping them conceal the evidence of their crime, such as by washing the bloodstains out of their clothes. While they were all incarcerated at the county's adult jail, Chavis tried to communicate with the boys and tamper with their testimonies, although he was caught in the act by guards. Several weeks after these attempts, the guards found a written note in Alex's trashcan. Apart from instructions on how to handle the case, the note also included statements of love and Chavis's assurances to Alex that he would "wait for him." Even though Chavis later denied having anything to do with this note, it was very unlikely that it was planted there by anyone else.

Following the boys' change in testimony in April 2002, in which they accused Chavis, he was charged with first-degree murder, in addition to arson, sexual battery, and evidence and witness tampering. Chavis's trial thus went underway separate from the King boys, and they both acted as witnesses in the process. Implicating Chavis, Alex said that Chavis was the one who wanted the boys to relocate to his home and that he told them this wouldn't be possible until Terry died. Alex's testimony further stated that Chavis came to his dad's house on the night of the murder to drive them away. After having them wait in the trunk of his car, Chavis then allegedly went into Terry's house, admitting that he killed Terry once he came back to the car.

As per the earlier decision, the sentence in Chavis's trial was to remain sealed until a verdict was reached in the process against Derek and Alex. Ultimately, the charges of sexual molestation against Chavis were dropped, but he was found guilty of false imprisonment, tampering with evidence, and being an accessory to murder. In total, he was sentenced to 35 years in prison, which is a sentence that he is still serving.

Process Epilogue and the King Family's Problems

The two concurrent trials shared many of the same witnesses, among them Derek and Alex. When Alex was on the stand as a witness for his own defense, he gave even more details about his relationship with Chavis. At this point, Alex also falsely testified that Chavis himself bludgeoned Terry with the baseball bat, not Derek. He went on to say that the brothers' initial testimonies were just rehearsed stories meant to protect Rick Chavis.

Both boys were eventually found guilty of second-degree murder and arson, which could have landed them in prison for 22 years to life just for the murder on top of 30 years for arson. This conviction, however, was then thrown out by the judge because of problems in the prosecution's methods. The defense and prosecution were ordered to enter into mediation and reach an agreement. This agreement came on November 14 of 2002, when the boys pled guilty to third-degree murder and arson as part of the deal. For these crimes, Derek and Alex got eight and seven years in prison, respectively. Today, they are both free men after having been released in 2008 and 2009.

Even though Terry King may not have abused his sons, the family situation was far from idyllic and had many problems. The boys' mother, Kelly Marino, was a dysfunctional individual and wasn't present for much of her children's lives. Terry met her in 1985, after which they spent eight years living together, during which time they had Alex and Derek. In the course of this relationship, Kelly got pregnant by another man, giving birth to twins.

Things escalated further in 1994 when Kelly simply left Terry and the boys, as well as her two other sons. Perhaps the pressures of motherhood had pushed her past the breaking point, but Kelly also had a history of substance abuse, mostly drug problems. Both of her twins ended up being adopted the following year. As for Derek and Alex, they were split up because Terry struggled to support two children on his own. Derek went to live with Frank Lay, a high school principal, and his wife, Nancy.

Derek's foster family would later give many important testimonies during the murder trials. Notably, Frank and Nancy testified that Derek begged them not to send him back home when they decided to stop being his foster parents. According to the Lays, Derek told them that Alex hated their dad and that he wanted him to die. Nancy told the court that Derek informed her about an ongoing plan to kill Terry.

The reason why the Lays eventually decided to stop fostering Derek in September 2001 was his increasingly troublesome behavior that they simply had no means to control. Derek started doing various drugs that he could get his hands on, and he showed a growing propensity to play with fire. These disturbing developments made the Lays worry about the safety of their biological children.

Alex, too, was given a foster family for a while, but that arrangement didn't work out either. Interestingly enough, Terry's mother testified that Alex was actually happy when he was sent back to live with his dad. Once Derek came back, things started to take a dark turn yet again, and the situation around the house quickly tensed up.

According to Kelly, Terry was a strict but fair, gentle, and devoted father who had much love for his boys. The brothers, especially Derek, felt differently. Derek's rebellious nature was perhaps mixed with estrangement to create a sense of alienation and intolerance toward his father. The alleged "stares," which the boys at one point described as systematic punishment where Terry would put them both in a room and stare them down, also made Derek feel threatened. On top of that, Derek hated living in containment and was diagnosed with ADHD and prescribed Ritalin. Terry took Derek off this medication in the time leading up to the murder.

Overall, Derek seemed to have a very aggressive and violent side that featured a deep resentment toward his father and toward life in general. Even music could make

Derek go into a fit of rage, which Terry tried to mend by removing the television set and other devices from the house. This, like other attempts by Terry to placate his son, often only made Derek even more frustrated.

CHAPTER THREE:

Joseph and Erik Menendez

The case of Joseph Lyle and Erik Galen Menendez was one of those cases where the reasons and motives behind the killings would eventually come to the surface and overtake the whole trial. The motive, which was initially chalked up to just greed and robbery, proved to be much more complex than everyone thought, and it had the potential to determine the difference between villain and victim in the whole grueling story. This still holds true to this very day and can be seen in retrospective discussions about the case.

The murderous acts that the Mendez brothers committed shook the upscale communities of Beverly Hills and the entire nation to the core. How this family, seemingly living the definition of the American Dream, could come to this bloody point has challenged the worldly outlook of many folks. On the surface, the Mendez family really seemed to have had it all, and they were considered to be the picture-perfect example of success. According to the brothers, it was what the outside world couldn't see that eventually drove Lyle and Erik to murder both of their parents in a manner so brutal that the police initially thought it was a mafia hit planned to send a message.

The Menendez Family Background

The brothers' father, Jose Enrique Menendez, was a Cuban who was born into an affluent Cuban family on May 6, 1944. In pre-revolution Havana, Jose's folks were an influential, prominent family with lots of wealth and power. They were known as being great in business and other spheres, such as sports. Jose's father made part of his fame and wealth thanks to a successful soccer career. Apart from being a rather famous soccer player, Jose's father was also a businessman, and he owned his own company. On the other hand, Jose's mother was a highly successful swimmer and part of Cuba's sports hall of fame. As athletes, Jose's parents were famous and respected, which brought a lot of perks for Jose and his sister.

Following the Cuban Revolution in the 1950s, many of the elites who enjoyed privileges and wealth under the military dictatorship of President Fulgencio Batista were forced to leave and seek their fortune elsewhere. From a very young age, young Jose was pushed by his parents to achieve excellence and success in all aspects of life, considering anything less unworthy of the family name. This would continue once he arrived in America in 1960 as a 16-year-old teenage boy. He initially left with his sister's fiancé, first settling with his aunt in Hazleton, Pennsylvania.

Even though he was young and just an immigrant, Jose Enrique Menendez was sure he would succeed. His family was perhaps overbearing at times, but they did instill a sense of confidence and an insatiable thirst for success in Jose. Jose's early life in the United States was nowhere near as privileged as that in pre-revolution Cuba, but this didn't dissuade him, and he was determined to reclaim his status in this new, opportune environment.

In the years that he had to spend in high school, Jose was highly successful and a great achiever. Due to his good grades and history in sports, Jose was able to secure an athletic scholarship, which enabled him to attend Southern Illinois University in Carbondale. This was a great way for Jose to propel himself forward since he could not afford to attend any of the Ivy League schools. During these early college days, Jose met Mary Louise Anderson, known among her friends as Kitty. Mary Louise Anderson was a pretty girl, an outstanding student, and a beauty pageant winner, which were only some of the things that made Jose feel this was the perfect girl for him. After some dating, the two got married in 1964, after which they relocated to

New York. While there, Jose acquired an accounting degree from Queens College.

After his graduation, Jose successfully passed the CPA test to become a certified public accountant, beginning his successful career in business. At this time, many of his virtues began to emerge, along with many flaws. Wherever he worked, Jose found great professional success and was known as intelligent, gifted, and above all, diligent. However, many also got to know Jose's darker side, believing him to be arrogant, rude, and overly strict with people, especially his subordinates. Jose expected nothing but the best at all times, which was too much to handle for some folks.

Jose and Mary had their first son, Joseph Lyle, in early 1968, while Erik was born in late 1970. After the birth of Lyle, the family relocated to New Jersey, which ended up being Erik's place of birth. After starting a family, Jose remained a workaholic and focused much of his time and effort on work, while his wife stayed home for the most part. Still, Jose was far from uninvolved in the lives of his sons, far from it. Jose was strict and highly demanding with his children, applying similar standards to those that his father had for him. Being a Menendez meant something, and Jose was devoted to ensuring that his children would amount to a lot. Jose was also noted as an unfaithful husband who had numerous extramarital indiscretions.

Jose's business career was going very well, however. Already by 1973, Menendez became the chief financial officer at the Hertz Corporation. He quickly advanced, thanks to his drive, insatiable ambition, and natural aggressiveness. As some of Jose's former business associates noted, he wasn't just outperforming others but also believed himself to be more intelligent than most other people. This was one of the reasons why Jose held others to such high standards and was known as a highly critical person who often voiced his criticisms of others with no hesitation.

Both Jose's career and family life took another turn in 1986 when he and the family moved to California, where he was given a job as a chief operating officer at RCA Records. During this time, Menendez began meeting many celebrities and other important figures from show business. This was how Jose made his initial inroads into the industry that would bring him and his family even more wealth and fame.

Both Erik and Lyle were talented athletes from an early age. Erik, for instance, was an outstanding tennis player, showing great promise during his high school year. At one point, Erik was ranked as the 44th player in the entire US, among players under eighteen years of age. Jose fostered these talents, and he sought to get his sons to advance their sports careers. This was one of the reasons why Jose enrolled his sons in the Princeton Day School, starting them on a fast lane to success that wasn't available to him when he was still a teenage immigrant in the US.

The Path to Murder

Jose's ultimate dream was for his sons to go to the prestigious Princeton University. He believed that by attending Princeton, Erik and Lyle would be even more successful than him and would enter the elite American establishment in a way that wasn't possible for him. Despite their athletic gifts, though, Erik and Lyle soon began slacking in school, and they both turned out to be less than ideal students. From early on, it was also clear that the boys weren't as driven and aggressive as their father.

Lyle, in particular, was a somewhat reserved and shy boy who excelled neither in his studies nor in making friends. Lyle would eventually make it to Princeton, but he would struggle right from the start. On the other hand, Erik was more outgoing and social than Lyle, but he, too, didn't put much effort into his studies. Their poor academic performance didn't sit well with their highly demanding father. Even when they excelled, the boys were hardly ever good enough, so every failure had even more weight because of it.

Jose was highly involved in this aspect of his children's lives. He considered it to be his responsibility and dream to make his sons as perfect as they could possibly be – masters of every trade. To that effect, Jose was involved with his children's schooling to a great degree, often trying to make sure that they were studying and doing their homework. Sometimes, this sort of control would lead to unpleasant situations, particularly during Jose's many surprise quizzes that the children would have to go through. Jose would menacingly get in his children's faces during these intense sessions and ask them questions, reprimanding or even hitting them when they got their answers wrong.

This gradually created a toxic atmosphere of fear and made the boys hate school even more. Above all, Erik and Lyle would eventually feel little more than fear toward their father. While a lot of people, particularly his business associates, had a lot of respect for Jose Menendez, some thought very little of him. According to Pamela Bozanich, the prosecutor in the subsequent murder trial of the Menendez brothers, many people who knew Jose considered him to be a horrible person.

Jose's wife had many difficulties in their marriage as well. There were times when Kitty had suspicions of her husband's infidelities, but there was little she could do other than seek therapy with a psychiatrist. The stress brought on by her husband's infidelity on top of his harsh temperament eventually brought Kitty into a state of depression and suicidal thoughts, which was why she sought professional help.

Despite all these internal problems, the Menendez family successfully maintained a façade of not just normalcy but happiness and complete success, especially when Lyle made it to Princeton. During this time, Jose was confident that he would succeed in his dream of establishing a powerful family in America, and he intended to leave his entire estate to his sons.

Jose continued climbing the ladder, and he eventually became the president of LIVE Entertainment (Artisan Entertainment), a video distribution company set up in Los Angeles. This new job was a major leap for Jose's career, bringing a salary of more than $1 million and many important connections. This was when the family relocated to the suburbs of LA. Things took a turn for the worse when Lyle was suspended from Princeton due to poor grades and frequent absences. This was only the beginning, though, and the Menendez brothers would soon begin to act up in more serious ways.

Even though they lacked for nothing in life, Erik and Lyle started to burglarize homes in their upscale neighborhood. After robbing two homes, the brothers made off with over $100,000 in cash and other valuables. After being stopped for speeding, the boys were caught with the stolen goods in their trunks and promptly arrested. This was a major embarrassment for Jose and his entire family, even more so than Lyle's suspension from Princeton. Nonetheless, Jose quickly reacted to the arrests and ensured that his sons were released. Being an adult at that time, Lyle faced most of the legal consequences and was dealing with the possibility of significant prison time. Jose instructed his younger son, Erik, to take the blame by lying to the police. Erik being a minor and Jose having paid off the victims of their burglaries, the boys were soon released.

The boys were released on probation, though, and Erik also had to see a court-ordered psychologist, Dr. Jerome Oziel. Before their sessions began, Jose struck a deal with Dr. Oziel to find out everything he would talk about with his son. The brothers eventually caught wind of this, and Erik stopped opening up to Dr. Oziel. The embarrassment that the burglaries had caused for Jose prompted him to move the family again, this time to the affluent area of Beverly Hills. The mansion that Jose bought on North Elm Drive was worth some $4 million.

Unfortunately for the family, problems continued as it became clear that Erik and Lyle were simply not what their father wanted them to be. Around this time, Jose had to come to terms with this fact, but this didn't mean he would accept his children's differences. On the contrary, Jose decided to rewrite his will and cut Erik and Lyle out of the inheritance, an estate worth some $14 million at that time. For Erik and Lyle Menendez, this was the final straw – the final among many straws that were only about to come to light following the gruesome events of August 20, 1989.

The Menendez Murders and Trial

The evening of the murders was supposed to be a quiet, lazy summer evening. Mr. and Mrs. Menendez were resting in the den of their Beverly Hills home after shark fishing with the family earlier that day. With the boys going out for the evening, the Menendez couple settled down for a movie night.

For the outside world, the bloody drama began around 11:47 p.m. on August 20, 1989, when a local police precinct received a disturbing 911 call in Beverly Hills. On the other end of the line, a panicked young man was telling the operator that someone had murdered both of his parents. This was Lyle giving the performance of his life, laying the blame on unknown perpetrators when, in fact, he and his brother had just expended fifteen 12-gauge shotgun rounds into their parents. Jose and Kitty weren't just murdered; they were massacred to a point where it was difficult to identify them.

Apart from the couple's mangled corpses, the crime scene also consisted of blood and brain matter on the walls and ceiling, leaving first responders stunned. The brutality of the murders initially led the police to view this as a killing related to organized crime. After calling the police, the brothers also called Mark Heffernan, their tennis coach, informing him that Jose had been murdered and asking him to come over. Heffernan arrived at the Menendez mansion after the police, stumbling upon an active crime scene. The two boys were soon taken downtown for questioning. The boys contributed to the theories of a mafia-related killing by offering similar ideas in their interrogations. They told the police that their parents might have been killed by members of the mafia Jose worked with.

Around 10 p.m. on the night of the murders, some neighbors reported hearing sounds that sounded like firecrackers coming from the Menendez mansion. As Erik and Lyle entered the room, the first shot was fired at the back of Jose's head from point-blank range. His wife, who had dozed off on the couch by that time, jumped upon hearing the shot, trying to get away. However, she was shot in the leg and slipped on the blood gushing from the wound. Kitty was then shot multiple times at point-blank range, taking shotgun rounds to her arms, chest, and face.

After killing their parents, Erik and Lyle shot them again, this time in their kneecaps, to give their crime the appearance of being related to organized crime. The brothers also sought to cover their tracks by disposing of the shotguns on Mulholland Drive. After that, they went to see *License to Kill* in a nearby movie theater in an attempt to give themselves an alibi for the night. The police arrived at the mansion shortly after Lyle's 911 call at 11:47 p.m.

In the time leading up to the murders, Mr. and Mrs. Menendez acted very differently from each other. While Jose was relaxed to a point where he frequently left the alarm off and the gate open, Kitty was reported as being very agitated and even paranoid. During the trial, it became known that Kitty was afraid that her sons were sociopaths and potentially dangerous. She even kept a rifle just in case and always made sure to lock her bedroom door at night.

The police had their suspicions about the Menendez Brothers right from the start, but they had no evidence of their involvement, and what little evidence they did have pointed away from the brothers, at least initially. Erik and Lyle acted unscrupulously in the months after the murders, living in extravagant luxury and catching a lot of attention with their excessive spending. Apart from taking trips overseas and paying for top-notch tennis coaching, the brothers also bought expensive watches, cars, and even entire businesses. All the while, both brothers lived in separate, expensive penthouses. As the prosecutors stated during the trial, Erik and Lyle had spent around a million dollars within six months of their parents' killing.

The brothers were only caught after Erik told his psychiatrist about the murders, and this only happened after Lyle threatened the psychiatrist, giving him a way around doctor-patient privilege and making him seek the help of the police. The brothers were finally arrested in March 1990, and one of the most controversial trials in recent memory then ensued. After some initial delays, the two brothers were officially indicted by the Los Angeles County grand jury in December 1992.

During the first trial, which had two hung juries, some shocking revelations came to light, and it turned out that the Menendez family had more skeletons in their closet than anyone imagined. Leslie Abramson, the lead defense attorney for both Menendez brothers, based her defense on the revelation that Jose Menendez was abusing his sons mentally, physically, and sexually their entire lives. Whereas the prosecutors believed the boys were motivated solely by greed, the defense alleged that they killed their parents to put an end to the abuse.

These revelations created a lot of sympathy for Erik and Lyle, especially since Court TV was broadcasting the trial in 1993. Millions of people got to see emotional confessions from the Menendez brothers, detailing the abuse that they had endured, and it was difficult to argue with their sincerity. Soon enough, the grizzly details of Jose's past indiscretions began to blur the line between killer and victim. During the second trial, which was less public on the orders of Judge Stanley Weisberg, the prosecution was ultimately successful. After much nationwide controversy, the Menendez brothers were sentenced in July 1996 to life without the possibility of parole. The California Court of Appeal upheld the sentence in February 1998 and the California Supreme Court in May of the same year.

CHAPTER FOUR:

Stacey Lannert

The case of Stacey Ann Lannert and the murder that she had committed in 1990 is a tale that took on a whole new form quite a while after everyone thought it was already over. Stacey killed her father, Tom Lannert, when she was just a teenager, and she would pay a severe price for her crime. The premeditated nature of the cold-blooded act reflected very harshly on Stacey's sentencing. But other facts perhaps didn't reflect enough, even though they should have.

Stacey's story would eventually become an example of a young woman who decided to take a stand against her abuser, even though that meant doing the unthinkable. The severity of Stacey's sentence was probably owed to the prosecution's successful argument that the motive was money, but, in time, opinions shifted. From a certain perspective, this is partly a story about injustice, although the unexpected epilogue did manage to perhaps right some wrongs. It's also a testament that even after the harshest and most tragic of times, life can be repurposed and made to have meaning again. Stacey eventually found a way to do this by helping others and helping herself heal and attain redemption.

Victim Turned Killer

Stacey Lannert shot her father twice on July 4, 1990, in St. John, Missouri. She recalled that her early childhood, before she turned eight, was relatively normal and that she looked to her father as a hero like any other child does. She was born in St. Louis in 1972, and she spoke of how she and her dad had a close relationship in the early years of her life. Stacey said that the relationship made her feel special and happy, but alcohol was always a present problem, and, with years, it only got worse.

Things took a turn for the worse when Stacey's parents, Tom and Deborah Lannert, divorced and Deb moved away to Guam. Tom began drinking long before that, though, and Stacey and her younger sister, Christy, could see him gradually devolve from a father and husband into a monster. Stacey's first encounter with abuse was when she noticed that her father was physically abusive with Christy while their parents were still married, but she was mostly spared this kind of treatment for a while.

This didn't last, however, and Tom eventually began to

focus on Stacey after she turned eight. The abuse soon began to take on a sexual form as well, and Stacey's life would be an endless nightmare from that point on. Tom struck fear in his daughters through the abuse, but he also explicitly threatened them to keep quiet. The girls maintained silence for many years, but signs of abuse were often visible. Stacey was nine the first time her father raped her. In time, she made attempts to tell her mother and even her babysitter that she was being raped, but a combination of fear and her lack of vocabulary and understanding to explain what she was going through stifled these attempts.

Stacey's mother, Deborah, also had extensive experience with abuse, both physical and sexual. She was the oldest of five children, and already by age eleven, her father started to molest her. Other members of Deborah's family were abused or were abusers themselves. Deborah was only eighteen when she met Tom Lannert and the two married after only three months of dating. The Lannert couple and their daughters were generally a regular middle-class family, and they moved around a few times, such as in 1979 when they relocated to Alhambra, Illinois. The neighbors who later testified generally described the Lannerts as a quiet family who mostly kept to themselves.

While sexually abusing his daughters, Tom didn't just threaten them but also manipulated them. There was a time when Stacey believed that her father's sexual abuse of her was normal or even a sign of preference. It took a while for her to realize something was fundamentally wrong with her relationship with her dad, with the final realization occurring in eighth grade. After that point, Stacey tried her best to avoid her father, although this hardly ever worked and sometimes only made her father angrier and more abusive, especially when he was drunk. Every time Stacey tried to resist or reacted in any negative way, Tom would get worse.

Eventually, Stacey was ridden with guilt, shame, and other self-deprecating feelings that often come with sexual abuse. In time, people around Stacey, including her mother, began to suspect that something was going on, particularly when they would see physical clues, but nobody ever did anything about it. The visible clues were not enough to prove the abuse to Deborah beyond a reasonable doubt, despite all the personal experience that she had with abuse.

Stacey was thirteen when her mother left and remarried, leaving her children entirely in Tom's care. Later on, after the whole ordeal unfolded, Deborah expressed her regret, and she claimed that she never expected anything tragic to happen, firmly believing that Tom loved his daughters and that he would protect them, not hurt them. While Tom had already abused his daughters, the torment got significantly worse after the divorce, as did his drinking.

After years of heightened abuse, Stacey moved away in her senior year of high school and settled with her mom and step-dad in Guam. Unfortunately, Christy, who was eleven at that time, was left behind with her abusive father. Tom most likely didn't sexually abuse Christy, but he was always violent with her. In the time after Stacey left, Christy would alternate between living with her father and her relatives while also occasionally spending time with her mom in Guam. Over time, Christy wanted Stacey to return home, and she told her that she was being abused. Stacey couldn't bear the thought of leaving her sister alone with the monster that Tom had become any longer, so she eventually returned.

It didn't take long for Tom to go back to his old habits, and he started to sexually molest Stacey again. Now older and having tasted freedom away from her father, Stacey was increasingly unwilling to endure Tom's torment any longer. Her pain slowly evolved into anger, and anger gave way to hatred. A will to resist and take back control started to emerge, eventually evolving into fantasies of violent action. In due time, Stacey lost all inhibition in her desire to see her father gone. She wanted him to go away, and, in no time at all, it became clear to her that this meant she would have to take drastic action.

Stacey began to obsess over the idea of killing Tom. Initially, this was just a fantasy that she would occasionally share with her friends, saying that she would like to either kill her father or have someone else do it for her. She thought about hiring a killer to do this, but she would need money for that. Stacey and Christy stood to inherit money from Tom, so this was a combination that Stacey certainly thought about. It meant that she could afford the murder contract and secure herself and her sister for the future. This plan seemed highly appealing, but it would eventually cost Stacey dearly during the trial.

Crime and Punishment

On the night when Stacey killed her dad, she and her sister were staying in a hotel room. However, they had a puppy that they left at home, and Stacey was concerned for the pet's safety while it was alone with Tom. The sisters went back home shortly after 4 a.m. to try and retrieve the dog. When they arrived, Stacey snuck into the house through an open basement window and slowly crept her way into the home.

Once Stacey entered the basement, she saw her father's rifle. Looking at the weapon, Stacey began thinking. Suddenly, she was overcome with the ideas that had been brewing in her mind for some time. At that moment, she knew this was the night when she would kill. She armed herself and made her way upstairs, where she saw her father sleeping on the couch. Stacey raised her rifle and shot Tom close to the shoulder, shattering his collarbone with the initial bullet. Awaking in utter shock and terror, Tom didn't realize what was happening and couldn't even figure out he had been shot.

In a bizarre sequence, Tom told Stacey to call the police. She, too, was in shock and began to comply automatically, starting to search for a phone. While looking for the phone, she started thinking again, and she reminded herself that Tom deserved to die. She then went back to the living room and shot her father in the head as he was lying on the couch, this time killing him instantly.

The day after the killing, Stacey was unsure of what she should do and confided in a friend with the details of her crime. The friend sympathized with her and helped her hide the evidence rather than reporting her to the police. They got rid of the murder weapon, and, sometime after that, Stacey called the police to report that she had found her father lying murdered in his home. Stacey didn't keep the story up for long, though, and she eventually decided to confess to Lt. Tom Schulte, telling him that she had murdered her father after enduring a lifetime of abuse and rape.

Stacey stood to inherit an estate of around $100,000. She had planned to use this to get her and Christy on track toward a happy future. After the confession, this dream was over, at least for Stacey. After her arrest, she was charged with first-degree murder, and the prosecution immediately went to work, building a case that Stacey had murdered her father in cold blood solely for the money.

Stacey's lawyer initially wanted to base the defense on insanity, utilizing the battered woman syndrome, taking into account the lifetime of abuse that Stacey had endured. The court partially limited this approach, allowing the defense to attempt to prove self-defense. This, of course, was highly problematic since Stacey wasn't in danger at the time of the killing, and her father had, in fact, been sleeping when she attacked him. This was Stacey's own testimony, so the self-defense claim was eventually thrown out by the court.

Apart from short-lived attempts to get rid of some evidence on the day after the murder, Stacey never made any real concerted effort to deceive the court or anyone else. Right after the arrest, she told the whole story exactly as it was, including her experiences of abuse. However, right from the start, her claims of abuse received very little attention, and the police immediately assumed that Stacey's sole motive was money. The investigators noted that Stacey had been using her father's credit cards and writing checks on his account. They also discovered what they called evidence of attempts to hire a killer to get rid of Tom.

Incriminating testimonies to that effect were taken into account, and the police had no qualms charging Stacey with first-degree murder. One such contact that the investigators identified was Ronald Barnett, whom the prosecutors named as a potential killer who Stacey tried to hire. According to the prosecutor, she even gave Ronald a firearm for the job, which he later sold. The investigation also implicated Christy in this conspiracy, charging her with conspiracy to commit murder in the first degree. She would eventually be sentenced to five years in prison after pleading guilty to this charge.

When Stacey testified during her trial, she explained her inner deliberation on whether she should shoot her father or not, implying reluctance. Her biggest fear, as she explained, was that her sister would have to go through the same ordeal as she did. The idea of Christy having to endure the same abuse helped Stacey make up her mind and pull the trigger. Marilyn Anne Hutchinson, a psychologist who testified for Stacey's defense, argued that Stacey had been suffering from a dissociative disorder at the time of the killings.

Hutchinson described Stacey as a deeply traumatized and terrorized abuse victim who her family, the school system, and everyone else failed. What also served Stacey's case was the fact that she had made attempts to tell her babysitter, her mom, and others about the ongoing abuse. Stacey's lawyer.

51

Chris McGraugh described the failure of all these people to react as a "conspiracy of silence." In the end, neither the self-defense nor the insanity arguments worked out and were thrown out by the judge. The jury found Stacey guilty as charged with first-degree murder, and she was sentenced to life in prison without the possibility of parole.

A Second Life

Even though the jury found Stacey guilty of first-degree murder, some of its members were shocked and appalled that the details and facts of Stacey's prolonged sexual and physical abuse were ignored. Many people were surprised by how harsh Stacey's sentence was, even among those who did believe that she killed Tom for the money. They believed that even if this was the case, the history of abuse must have played a part in getting the relationship to a point where it was possible for Stacey to be in a state of mind needed to kill her father.

Stacey and her lawyers would file multiple appeals over the years but to no avail. At the Missouri Court of Appeals, for instance, the judge supported the original trial judge. At the US Court of Appeals for the Eighth Circuit, Stacey's appeal was thrown out, but the court's statement showed understanding for her case. In it, the court described it as troubling that the original jury was not fully informed about the true scope of abuse that Stacey had gone through in childhood. What's more, the Missouri self-defense statute does not outline a specific timeframe between the attack and the self-defense. In simple terms, this meant that Stacey's self-defense claim might well have worked had the jury been properly introduced to the facts of her abuse at the hands of Tom. As such, even though the court ruled against Stacey's appeal in 2003, it did so "reluctantly."

After her appeals failed multiple times and in different courts, Stacey had few options still open to her. Eventually, she turned to Matt Blunt, the Governor of Missouri at the time, hoping to have her sentence commuted at least to life with the possibility of parole after fifteen years served. This was at a point where Stacey had already served eighteen years of her sentence. In the best-case scenario, Stacey was hoping for a pardon.

Stacey's big break came in 2009 when Governor Matt Blunt was on his way out. As one of his final acts, he announced that he was commuting Stacey Lannert's sentence after having conducted an "exhaustive review" of all the facts in her case. Governor Blunt did the same for another woman, Charity Carey, who was in a similar situation. Blunt noted that these women simply took action against men who raped them and who abused them horribly for years. Stacey was eligible for release based on time already served, and she soon had her freedom on January 16 of 2009.

Bob McCulloch, the St. Louis County prosecutor, never changed his mind about the case. After her release, he said that former Governor Blunt should be ashamed of himself and that Stacey Lannert was nothing but a manipulator and a liar who murdered her father solely for the inheritance. He called into question her story of abuse and said that she should have spent the rest of her days in prison. McCulloch did acknowledge that Tom was a bad father and a drunkard, but he believed there was no evidence that he raped his daughter. McCulloch even commented that if Stacey had really been raped, she would have tried to get away from home, which, in reality, she did when she moved away to Guam and tried to get her sister to join her.

Stacey later expressed her regret that she killed her father before he got the chance to repent and change his ways. Still, she has always reiterated that her main wish was for Tom to leave her alone and to make sure that nothing would happen to her sister. At the time, murder was the only way she saw of getting this done. Beyond her crime of patricide, Stacey was never known to be problematic or violent, which she had shown in prison as well through her good behavior.

In prison, Stacey began to participate actively in various

projects helping victims of incest and all sorts of abuse get their lives back on track. She has continued on this path since she was released, and then some. Stacey later founded Healing Sister, a non-profit organization that helps women who have survived experiences similar to what she had to endure. Stacey has since acquired degrees in psychology and law, both of which have helped her vastly improve her work in this field. Stacey has also been hosted on various TV shows such as The Oprah Winfrey Show and others and has even published her memoirs in 2011, under the title of *Redemption: A Story of Sisterhood, Survival, and Finding Freedom Behind Bars.*

CHAPTER FIVE:

Esmie Tseng

In another shocking matricidal episode, 16-year-old Esmie Tseng deeply disturbed her peaceful community of Overland Park, Kansas, when she stabbed her mother to death in 2005. Esmie was an honor student and among the best classical pianists in the state. A model child, Esmie worked hard, and she was pushed hard – perhaps too hard as things turned out.

Esmie's mother, 55-year-old Shu Yi Zhang, just like her husband, Tao Tseng, was a strict parent who demanded a lot from her child. Esmie was not expected to perform well or excellently, she was expected to perform flawlessly. Esmie's mother's demands and her methods of ensuring that those demands were met often veered into cruelty. When Esmie would fail to meet the criteria, she would be subjected to various punishments that could easily classify as abuse. Scoring 96% on an exam was considered an utter failure by Shu Yi, and it would result in punishment, humiliation, and endless emotional torment.

On the surface, the model child was the picture of success. What the outside world didn't see was the price of that success. Her parents' extraordinarily high expectations greatly strained Esmie's mental health, and her state gradually deteriorated. All of this would culminate in a severe altercation that spiraled into a bloody crescendo as Esmie took a knife to her mother.

Esmie's Life

"I've been trying to make them smile, make them feel better, take Esmie off their list of worries and concerns." These were some of the last words that Esmie ever wrote about her parents in an online diary she kept keeping in the months leading up to the tragedy on August 19, 2005. That last entry was made some ten days before Esmie stabbed her mother to death.

One of the fathers from the local community, Jacob Horwitz, testified how shocked his kids were by the revelation. His children knew Esmie, and they went to summer camp with her, at which time she was a child that any parent would have been proud of, as Horwitz put it. Jacob's kids told him that they just couldn't believe the news as they were watching it, saying that Esmie had been arrested in connection to her mother's brutal killing. They described her as very pleasant and easy to get along with.

Esmie was never known to get in trouble, and other kids' parents were always happy to learn that their children were keeping such company, including Horwitz.

Jacob later went on to describe how he went online shortly after hearing the news of the killing, hoping to learn more about the case. This was when he found one of Esmie's online blogs that she used as a journal. It took him several hours to read all of her writings, and he learned that Esmie had been a deeply troubled girl for quite a while. She complained about various issues, but the central problem seemed to be Esmie's parents and their unbearably high and strict standards. Esmie's parents, who were Chinese immigrants, considered it a crucial question of honor to ensure that their child was the absolute best in all her academic pursuits.

Esmie loved playing the piano, and she was incredibly gifted, yet her parents used even that to threaten and terrorize her. Losing in state competitions, for instance, could have resulted in her piano being sold, which was a threat that laid heavily on Esmie's mind. Esmie's parents wouldn't just ground her or take things away from her. Sometimes, when she performed below the standards they had set out for her, Esmie's parents would have her stand naked in a corner for extended periods.

All of this pain and suffering was invisible to most of

the outside world, which was why the murder of Shu Yi Zhang was so shocking to the entire community. Zhang's friends, for example, didn't have much to go on other than gossip and news articles. None of them could make sense of what happened, as they knew Esmie to be a golden child and Zhang to be a responsible, normal woman. Way, one of Zhang's friends and colleagues, noted how Zhang seemed happy in the time before her death, giving no indication that anything was going wrong. Of course, she also pointed out that it was an aspect of Chinese culture to hide family difficulties from the public eye, so even though the relationship between Zhang and her daughter might have been deteriorating, it would have been difficult to tell for an outsider.

Yalu Pao, a mother of three from the same community, later commented how the Sino-American cultural divide could sometimes make it difficult for Chinese parents to raise their kids in America. As she explained, Chinese immigrant parents often have issues with their children who are born in America because Chinese culture and traditions revolve a lot around discipline that's expected of children. American culture is much more open, and children are afforded much more freedom by society than is normal in China.

Beyond her occasional complaints, which now seem

much more ominous after the fact, much of Esmie's online journal was normal for a teenager, although it gradually got darker. A lot of it had to do with music, socializing, and other things that kids her age are interested in. In time, she began to talk more and more about things like mental illness and sadness. Esmie expressed her suspicions that there might be something wrong with her mental health, but she also explained that she avoided seeking help because she was afraid of what she might learn about herself. She also began to write more and more about existential topics, the meaninglessness that she had perceived in life, and her feelings of hopelessness.

Already in early 2004 – a year and a half before the murder of Zhang – Esmie wrote about her deteriorating mental health in more detail than ever. She complained that she wished someone would help her "shut up" her brain and the recurring, troublesome thoughts that wouldn't leave her alone. Not only that, but she was also having trouble sleeping, which made matters a whole lot worse. After a while, Esmie would write that she felt as if she had become a stranger to herself.

One of the incidents that almost pushed Esmie over the edge the first time was when her parents threatened to move because she had three B's on a report card. Esmie was highly sociable, and she had many friends, some of whom were very close, and this threat infuriated her no end. In light of these threats, Esmie wrote in one of her journals that she was afraid of what she "might resort to." Speaking about her parents, she wrote that they were forcing her to "become indifferent to conscience."

The Descent

The neighborhood where Esmie lived was quiet and idyllically suburban American. While the problems that Esmie was having at home remained mostly hidden from the outside world, small hints would pop up here and there, as later described by Esmie's friends and acquaintances. These hints, however, could often be interpreted as relatively normal or just quirky at worst, not really testifying to the borderline abuse that Esmie was going through. For instance, Esmie's friends remember that her family was very protective of her, which was generally chalked up to her being an only child.

This protectiveness did occasionally veer off into peculiar territory, though. For example, when Esmie wanted to visit a new friend at their home, her father would go there first to make sure that the family didn't keep any dangerous pets. Esmie's friends also testified that her parents had a way of blaming her for their issues in life. Her mother blamed her for being laid off from an earlier job, even though Esmie had nothing to do with it. Another one of her friends, Katie, described how Esmie's mom would sometimes leave mean, hand-written notes on her computer, calling her lazy, disappointing, and telling her that she was ashamed to have her as a daughter.

Whereas other girls or even boys could be driven to tears by such words from their parents, especially during the sensitive teen years, Esmie reacted quite differently. In fact, she hardly reacted at all, except for when she would correct the grammatical and spelling mistakes on the notes before giving them back to her mother, perhaps as an act of minor revenge.

Esmie's father, too, had moments when he would belittle his daughter. Esmie wrote about one such instance on Christmas Eve in 2003, when she got her only Christmas gift from the neighbors who stopped by to give it to her. During their brief visit, the neighbors commented on Esmie's medals, which she had won in math competitions, saying that she was a genius. Hearing this, Esmie's father's first response was, "Definitely not."

Things culminated on that fateful day in August 2005 when something probably snapped in Esmie's mind. The police believed that the altercation – probably just the latest of many such incidents – led to a physical struggle that went on throughout the house, in multiple rooms. A knife eventually found its way into the fight and, at the end of the ordeal, Shu Yi Zhang was lying dead in a pool of blood, stabbed and hacked to death with a butcher's knife. Not many other details of the actual murder would make it to the public.

Jacob Horwitz theorized that the conflict began and turned physical, most likely in the kitchen, given that Esmie ended up using a kitchen knife as a murder weapon. Despite expressing considerable rage in her online journals, Esmie didn't have a history of physical violence, so whatever happened during the fight must have been extraordinarily upsetting. It was either that or Esmie had simply reached a breaking point where that final straw didn't even have to be particularly heavy. Whatever it was that the investigators found at the crime scene was certainly gruesome enough to motivate the District Attorney to ask for Esmie to be tried as an adult.

Sometime before the murder, in late July 2005, Esmie had a bit of a run-in with the cops. She had visited the local Temple B'nai Jehudah, where she had only visited once before in her life. Esmie dropped by around 6 p.m. as Rabbi Neal Schuster was beginning his sundown service with a congregation. Schuster later described how even though he had never seen Esmie before, he could tell something was very wrong with her. This was even before she started to put out the Rabbi's candles in the middle of his service. Schuster asked her if she needed to talk to someone, to which she said yes and was then escorted outside.

Esmie told the Rabbi and a couple of other members of the congregation that she had decided to run away from home. Strangely enough, Esmie also told them that she was hearing voices in her head, which told her to put out the Rabbi's candles. Since Esmie was a minor, the police were soon called, and they sent a patrol to take Esmie home. The responder was Officer Catherine Kamler from the Juvenile Unit of the Overland Park Police Department. Officer Catherine was doing her job according to textbook procedure when she brought Esmie home. Not even in her wildest dreams could she anticipate that Esmie would be arrested at that same home the following month for the murder of her own mother.

It wasn't long after her arrest and the beginning of the legal process that Esmie began to draw in a lot of sympathy. Parents but also other kids from the local community and beyond started to show a lot of interest in her case, signing petitions and sending letters of support to Esmie. Even websites dedicated to supporting Esmie started to pop up, such as the website put together by Jacob Horwitz. Many of these people would attend Esmie's hearings and other court proceedings, giving her much more support than she received from her father.

Proceedings and Controversies

The most immediate issue with the trial was whether Esmie would be tried as an adult. Her father, Tao, was remarkably slow to react and try to help his underage daughter. Instead of reacting right away, he waited some two months before he issued a statement in which he asked for her to be tried as a juvenile. He didn't come to Esmie's first hearing and only started frequenting her trial sessions after that first hearing. Friends of the family later said that the first thing Tao did after his daughter was arrested for the murder of his wife was to sell Esmie's piano.

In the end, Johnson County District Attorney Paul Morrison was successful in his pushes to have Esmie Tseng tried as an adult. Esmie was generally as composed and seemingly indifferent as ever. She pleaded guilty to voluntary manslaughter in March 2006, not long before her 17th birthday. Early on, a deal was struck between the prosecution and defense to go for a sentence of 100 months, amounting to less than nine years. This was only to be a recommendation made to the judge, with the ultimate decision being left to the judge's discretion.

Once it became clear that Esmie would be tried as an adult, it became likely that she would serve any eventual sentence in the Topeka Correctional Facility for Women, a regular adult prison. The defense, as well as Esmie's supporters, argued that putting her in prison alongside adult convicts was dangerous since she was a minor and just a teenage girl with no prior history of violence. The District Attorney believed the opposite, pointing out that the nature of her heinous crime was gruesome enough to show that Esmie was more than capable of violence and was thus more likely to be a threat to others than a victim.

Morrison did acknowledge the cruel treatment that Esmie had endured at the hands of her mother as well as her youth, but he stressed that "hacking someone to death with a butcher knife is about as serious as it gets." In his view, the problems she had with her parents were nowhere near enough to excuse her actions. The prosecutor's fear was that if she ended up in the juvenile correctional system, Esmie could have been released within months. He and others felt this would have been unfair given the severity of her crime despite the extenuating circumstances.

Many of the activists and organizations dealing with human rights strongly disagreed, though. According to Alison Parker, a senior researcher at the US branch of the Human Rights Watch in New York, treating Esmie as an adult in the first place was highly problematic. Parker argued that this shouldn't be determined based on the severity of the crime since even young children can often be capable of committing a crime just as violent as an adult.

Alison didn't get involved too much in Esmie's particular case, but she did point to it as yet another in a string of examples of a growing number of juveniles being treated as adults by the US justice system. At the time of the trial in 2006, there were some 9,700 American citizens in prison after being sentenced as adults for crimes that they had committed while they were juveniles.

Some of the greatest controversies surrounded the questions of motive and whether Esmie was a genuinely bad person or just a good kid who couldn't take her parents' abusive perfectionism any longer. The local community and the public, in general, were so invested in the case that court employees and deputies of the Johnson County Sheriff's Office had to kick excess people out of the courtroom. People were trying to get in and bring their friends, attempting to sit on each other's laps as there was no room in the small courtroom at the Johnson County Courthouse.

Particularly committed were Esmie's friends from Blue Valley North High School. Esmie certainly showed appreciation for this support, visibly smiling at her friends who were outside the courthouse. She seemed to enjoy her time in the courtroom much more than in detention, thanks to the support she got.

Jacob Horowitz was an especially distinguished

supporter and viewed by many as a sort of leader for the supporters. He was strongly committed to the belief that it was wrong to treat Esmie as an adult, and he kept trying to petition the court against this decision for as long as possible. These efforts were led by his organization called Friends of Esmie, using Esmie.com as a public platform.

Horowitz wasn't the activist type prior to Esmie's case, just like many other supporters who were moved by her story. In the end, the efforts of the supporters to get the court to treat Esmie as a juvenile were unsuccessful, but the deal between the prosecution and defense did help keep Esmie's ultimate sentence within reasonable bounds. In the end, she was found guilty of voluntary manslaughter, not murder, and she served a sentence of eight years and four months. Since October 1 of 2012, Esmie Tseng has been a free woman.

CHAPTER SIX:

Sarah Marie Johnson

The Johnson killings happened in Idaho in 2003. Diane and Alan Scott Johnson were upstanding members of their community in the small Idaho town of Bellevue. They enjoyed a solid reputation in the community and were also a fairly successful family living in a beautiful home in the suburbs. Alan was a businessman and partial owner of a very prosperous landscaping company, while Diane was employed in a financial company. The Johnsons were regarded as a happy couple highly devoted to their two children – a boy and a girl.

The couple had been married for 20 years at the time when they died at the hands of their daughter, Sarah Marie Johnson. Sarah was sixteen when she shot her parents with a high-power bolt-action rifle on September 2 of 2003. The shooting was a bloody affair that produced a rather gruesome crime scene in the home, and, initially, Sarah seemed to be just a terrified victim. The case would receive a lot of attention in time, being featured on television and in films on numerous occasions. In regard to motive and a few other aspects, the crime was similar to the killings of the Richardson family.

Romance and Obsession

The Johnson killings were another example of parricide resulting from the forbidding of love. Sarah was sixteen and seeing a 19-year-old boy. Her parents didn't approve of him, not just because of his age but also his background and bad influence. When they tried to put a stop to this relationship, nobody had any idea that a brutal double-murder was about to happen as a result and destroy an entire family.

The boyfriend was a Mexican man named Bruno Santos, an illegal immigrant in the US. He was a poor boy from a poor family and eventually dropped out of high school. With few prospects from that point on, Santos increasingly engaged in illegal activities and spent most of his time in the streets, involved with narcotics. It wasn't just Sarah's parents who disapproved of her relationship with Santos but her wider family as well.

Indeed, Santos was the object of many debates and arguments among family members and relatives alike. Sarah's friends didn't have many positive things to say about Santos either. Syringa Stark, for instance, was one of Sarah's friends, and she later testified that she always felt Sarah could and should do much better than Santos, noting that he was a drug dealer, whereas Sarah came from a family that was a pillar of its community.

A significant escalation in this whole drama came during the 2003 Labor Day weekend just before the murders. On Saturday, Sarah's parents were outraged to find out that she was sleeping over at Bruno's place, and her father went there to pick her up and bring her home immediately. There was a brief altercation, and Alan told Santos to stay away from his daughter, threatening him with the police, which were threats that he would never get to follow through on.

Linda Vavold, Sarah's aunt, gave detailed testimonies about this day during the subsequent murder trial because she and her husband, James, were staying with the Johnsons that weekend. James went along with Alan when he found out that his daughter had lied about her whereabouts to stay with Santos. After the confrontation at Santos' apartment, the Vavolds left so the Johnsons could try to settle things with their daughter. They returned not long afterward, and they found that Sarah was very angry, constantly pouting, and refusing to cooperate in any way. Meanwhile, the family tried to salvage what was left of their plans for Labor Day weekend.

Sarah later said that she spent most of the time

that weekend in the guesthouse, studying and doing homework, although the Vavolds cast some doubt on that since she never brought over any of her books. According to prosecutors, this was when Sarah concocted her hellish plan and premeditated the murder of her parents. The murder weapon that Sarah would use, which was a .264 Winchester Magnum rifle, belonged to Mel Speegle, the person renting the guesthouse who was absent at that time.

Alan never got to follow through on his threats to report Santos to the police because he was killed along with Diane on Tuesday morning. That morning, the police received an emergency call placed by Sarah from a neighbor's house, saying that a burglar had just shot her parents. When the cops arrived at the Johnson residence, they found a horrific crime scene. Blaine County Sheriff Walt Femling gave a detailed account of what he and his deputies saw. He remembered bits of hair and a lot of blood on the carpet, the ceiling, and the walls.

A part of Diane's skull cap flew away as she was shot point-blank and ended up in the hallway. The shot utterly destroyed a significant portion of her face. Alan was taking a shower at the moment when Diane was shot in the head as she slept, and he immediately came out of the bathroom to investigate. That's when he was shot in the chest. Tracks left in a mixture of water and blood showed that Alan was able to take a few steps toward Diane's bed after he was shot, but he eventually collapsed and bled out. The police found Diane in her blood-soaked bed and Alan lying dead on the floor not far away from her.

The police secured the crime scene and cordoned off the area around the house to preserve any evidence that might have been left outdoors, particularly the trash. In fact, a garbage truck had already passed through the neighborhood, so the police had to catch up with the waste disposal company, which eventually led to the discovery of key evidence.

Nobody suspected Sarah of murder at this point, while some folk cast the blame on Santos. Relatives and family members soon learned of what had happened, and they came to offer their support. As far as everyone was concerned, in the immediate aftermath of the killings, Sarah was a victim orphaned by a vicious attacker who intruded into her home.

Investigation

It didn't take long for Sarah to begin arousing suspicions with strange behavior and bizarre attitudes regarding the whole gruesome affair. Some of the key pieces of evidence that the investigators found included a bloody bathrobe, a left-hand leather glove and a right-hand latex glove. These items were found to contain DNA traces, which the cops expected to belong to the victims and the perpetrator, most likely Bruno Santos. Another suspect was the guesthouse tenant based on the murder weapon, but this was quickly ruled out because he had a full alibi.

Furthermore, the initial crime scene investigation unveiled a trail of blood, bits of tissue, and bone fragments leading from the bedroom where the couple was slain, across the hallway, and all the way to Sarah's bedroom. The cops also found the rifle in the master bedroom and two butcher's knives on the edge of the Johnson's bed. To make matters worse for Sarah, additional ammunition for the Winchester rifle was found in her bedroom. Also problematic for Sarah's claim of intruders was the fact that there were zero signs of forced entry onto the premises.

Both the police and family relatives began to notice that Sarah was acting rather strangely. Especially notable were her coldness and an apparent lack of interest in any of what was going on. Sheriff Femling was the first to notice this, and he told his investigative team to take note of Sarah's demeanor as a potential clue. He found it particularly strange how this 16-year-old girl didn't run away and hide or lock herself in her room in shock. Instead, she sat on the fence outside and watched as police and EMTs brought the corpses of her parents out in body bags.

Sarah's friends got the same feeling from her, noting that her grief didn't seem genuine at all. For instance, some of their parents testified that it was bizarre how Sarah focused on things like appointments with her nail and hair stylists instead of grieving. A friend of Sarah's by the name of Change Caudle remembered the exact moment when she realized that Sarah had killed her parents. Sarah came up to her during volleyball practice and told her to tell Santos that she loved him no matter what happened in the future.

The police became more suspicious as they questioned a growing number of relatives and friends. Once they learned about the altercations involving Santos and the strained relationship between Sarah and her parents, they took samples of her DNA and her fingerprints. During Sarah's first round of questioning, she told the investigators that she woke up around 6:15 in the morning and heard that one of her parents was showering. As she lay in bed, she heard gunshots and jumped up to run to her parents' room. She saw that their door was closed and she tried knocking and calling her mother. After receiving no answer, she alleged, an ominous feeling of fear washed over her, and she ran away to call for help, screaming as she exited her house.

This story changed soon, though, and it wouldn't be the last time. The more Sarah talked to the police, the more contradictions began to emerge. She often contradicted herself in regard to the door to her parent's bedroom, which she sometimes said was open, while at other times, it was closed. She also mixed up her own door with that of her parents on numerous occasions. The police had physical evidence, though, and it indicated that both doors were open at the time of the killings.

When the cops asked her about the pink robe that they found in the trash, Sarah's immediate response was a bizarre, unprovoked denial of guilt, in which she just said that she didn't kill her parents. She admitted that the robe belonged to her, but she said she had no clue how it ended up outside or who threw it in the trash. One of her theories was that a maid recently fired after she was caught stealing from the house had perpetrated the crime.

A break in the case came when the police received the results of the DNA analysis of the samples retrieved from the robe and the gloves. Unsurprisingly, the blood on Sarah's robe belonged to Diane, and other DNA traces on it were Sarah's. Worse yet for Sarah, the leather glove that the cops found contained gunpowder residue on the outside and Sarah's DNA on the inside. Finally, the socks Sarah wore on the morning of September 2 had traces of Diane's blood. By October 29 of 2003, Sarah was apprehended and charged with two counts of first-degree murder.

Legal Outcome

During the whole ordeal, Sarah's older brother Matt was away at college. After the turbulence that occurred during Labor Day weekend, both Diane and Alan called Matt to tell him about what had happened. Diane complained to Matt about his sister, telling him how disappointed she was and what a strain on the family her relationship with Bruno had been. This was on the night before the murders, and Matt later testified that his mother cried during the call. Matt also talked to Sarah, who seemed indifferent toward being grounded and somewhat ominously told Matt that she knew what her parents were up to. This was unlike Sarah, who would usually react strongly to being punished. Matt later said that he even thought about calling his mother back, but it was already late, so he changed his mind. He would never get a chance to talk to his parents again.

At the trial, the prosecution had to rely heavily on the evidence the police found in the trash. However, there were problems with the items. In regard to the robe, for instance, a lot of the blood on it was actually on the back, which was difficult to explain. Some of the blood was also soaked into the left sleeve. Sarah's defense lawyer, Bob Pangburn, was well aware of this hole in the prosecution's case, and he intended to make use of it. He implied that the presence of the blood on the back of the robe that Sarah was supposedly wearing while committing the murders indicated that the evidence might have been contaminated in the course of the investigation.

The lawyer made these comments while appearing as a guest on Nancy Grace's *Current Affairs*. The host theorizes that Sarah might have purposely put the robe on backward to use as a shield against blood splatter, ending up anywhere on her body. This idea was actually adopted by the prosecution, whose lawyers happened to be watching the show. The defense made a terrible mistake discussing the ongoing trial so publicly, and this would prove to be a serious problem for their case later on.

Something else that was very important for the prosecution was Sarah's behavior in the aftermath of the killings. A significant portion of the trial's testimonies revolved around how Sarah reacted to the tragedy, including various observations by family and friends. Many people considered it inappropriate at the very least, while some were convinced that this proved her guilt. Others just thought that she might have been sociopathic. Those who expressed their condolences to Sarah on the day of the murders noted that she wasn't traumatized and showed no emotions other than wanting to see her boyfriend. Her displays of indifference continued at the funeral, where she was heard talking about playing volleyball in the evening.

Her "grief" as her parents were being laid to rest had failed to convince a single person present.

Sarah's defense suffered a powerful onslaught from her brother's testimony. Matt began by describing his sister as a "drama queen," and, worse yet, he said that she was an excellent actor who liked to tell lies. He spoke for two hours and described what happened when he came home after hearing the horrible news. He said that the first thing Sarah told him was that she was a suspect, clearly showing that self-interest was her priority. Matt expressed his suspicion that Bruno might have done it, but Sarah denied this by saying that he loved Alan, which Matt didn't believe for a second. Nobody else did either, particularly after taking into account the altercation between Bruno and Alan during the Labor Day weekend. Despite believing that Bruno might have perpetrated the killings, Matt still had his suspicions that Sarah was at least an accomplice and, as he told the court, this was why he avoided asking her questions. He was afraid to hear the truth.

One thing that certainly bolstered Sarah's case was how clean she and her clothes were, with no traces of matter, tissue, or blood relating to the crime whatsoever. The investigators thoroughly examined her hair, hands, and other areas that are likely to catch blood splatter in a murder case like this. Experts were brought in, and they testified that it was virtually impossible to kill Diane the way she had been killed and not be sprayed with blood, at least on a microscopic level. And yet, the police examined Sarah for such cases on the very day of the murder. Although the murder weapon had one unidentified fingerprint, it couldn't be positively matched with Sarah's prints. There were also no prints on any of the bullets or the butcher knives found at the scene.

Also incriminating were the comments that Sarah had made to her cellmates regarding how she had placed the knives on the bed to throw off the investigation and mislead the police. The defense made the argument that these comments were inadmissible because Sarah was a minor and, as such, shouldn't have been incarcerated with adults. The judge threw these objections out on the grounds that Sarah was already being tried as an adult. The defense even tried to accuse Matt Johnson of trying to remove his sister so he could get her life insurance.

None of these attempts worked, and the jury eventually found Sarah guilty of two counts of first-degree murder after eleven hours of deliberation. The judge passed down the sentence of two terms of life in prison plus another fifteen years, all without the possibility of parole. For good measure, the judge also fined Sarah $10,000, half of which was to be paid to Matt Johnson.

Sarah and her lawyers would later make attempts to appeal the sentence, first in 2011 and then in 2012 when a hearing was granted in November. The hearing was granted on the basis of technological advancements in regard to DNA and fingerprint use, which had advanced significantly since the original trial. The appeal was ultimately rejected in February of 2014. Sarah is still serving her sentence at Pocatello Women's Correctional Center in Idaho, and she has never admitted to herparricide. The one thing that must have changed was her blind, youthful love for Bruno, who, in the end, testified against her during the trial.

CHAPTER SEVEN:

Thomas Gilbert

In yet another example of trouble in paradise, Thomas Gilbert Jr. was a well-to-do hedge fund heir and Princeton graduate who murdered his own father. The parents, Thomas and Shelley, were very successful in the financial sector and were working to ensure that their children would follow the same path of success. Instead of this path, Thomas Jr. chose one that would make him forever known as the Ivy League Father Killer. The Gilbert family had been successful for generations, so Thomas Jr. was undoubtedly born into a life of luxury, privilege, and opportunity.

In her 911 call reporting the killing to the police, Shelley was recorded as saying that she had been aware for some time that her son was "nuts" but that he had now crossed a threshold that she didn't see coming. The killing was a relatively recent case that occurred in January of 2015. The case received a high degree of media attention, leading to much speculation and debate as to the true underlying motive for the killing. The defense's attempts to go the insanity route during the trial ultimately didn't work, leading the public discourse in the direction of universal condemnation of Thomas Jr., whose crime was referred to by the prosecutors as the ultimate tantrum.

The Gilbert Family

Thomas Sr. was born in 1945 into an already affluent family that had him on a path toward success and riches right from the start. After receiving his base education in exclusive prep schools, he went on to study at numerous Ivy League universities, acquiring degrees from Princeton and Harvard. After finishing his formal education, Gilbert went to work on Wall Street, where he was very successful in investment. More importantly, this was when he met and married Shelley Stevens Rea, who worked as an assistant VP at the New Court Securities Corporation at the time.

The young Gilbert couple easily made their way as distinguished New York socialites. As individuals of great renown and with many connections, both Thomas and Shelley were written into the Social Register, along with members of other wealthy, influential families. This formalized the couple's position in New York's high society. Apart from their reputation, connections, and money, the Gilbert couple also owned several homes around New York.

Thomas Jr. came into their life when he was born in

1984, followed by his sister Clare not long afterward. Shelley could afford to suspend her professional pursuits temporarily in the interest of motherhood, and she spent the following period of her life focusing on her children. Thomas Jr., or Tommy as he was commonly called, grew into a handsome boy who seemed to be firmly set on following in his father's footsteps. Tommy was handsome, highly athletic, and he received the best educational opportunities, setting him on a path to become part of the elite.

The ideas and plans for the future that Tommy had for himself started to diverge from those of his father when it was time for Tommy to start working. Instead of beginning by working at his father's firm as Thomas Sr. wanted, Tommy sought to venture out on his own and be an independent businessman. He wanted to do this without his family's assistance, but this was a difficult road that he was perhaps not ready for. Tommy's business endeavors struggled to take off, and he found himself leaning on his parents time and time again. While he found it difficult to succeed in his endeavors, Tommy was also a high spender at the same time, preferring to live in upscale neighborhoods and having to pay high monthly rent. To help him stay afloat, his parents set up a weekly allowance of $1,000 for him.

Tommy didn't put much effort into finding out where the problems were or coming up with a new approach to making his businesses prosper. He spent a lot of his free time surfing, going to parties, and hanging out with the other socialites of New York. Tommy found himself fitting into the socialite scene, but only on the surface level. He was from a wealthy family, he was handsome, tall, and had style, but he had other problems under the surface. Later on, witnesses described him as aloof, awkward, erratic, and even prone to violently lashing out.

Over time, it became increasingly clear that Tommy was turning out to be a disappointment to his father and the rest of the family. Gradually, the distance between Tommy and his folks started growing. One indication of this was an email that Tommy had sent to his father in late 2013, more or less telling him that the more distant they were, the better. As vocal as he was in his desire to be as far away from his father as possible, Tommy did little in the way of achieving financial independence to support that distance on his own. In fact, he would remain financially dependent on his parents for quite a while to come.

Tommy preferred to live lavishly at the expense of his parents than to work for a living. He could have tried harder to make it on his own, but he also always had the option of falling back in line and working with his father. Neither of these seemed to interest Tommy enough to keep him motivated and going the right course. In time, Thomas Sr.

began to reduce his son's allowance in an attempt to bring him back into the fold. By the time of the final altercation and murder, when Thomas Sr. threatened to cut Tommy off completely, his allowance had decreased from the initial $1,000 a week to around $300.

Things would reach a boiling point on January 4 of 2015, when Tommy came unannounced to his parents' home in Manhattan. Shelley later recalled how happy she was to see her son and that she was glad to hear that he wanted to speak to his father about "business." In her mind, this was great news because she thought that Tommy was finally coming around and getting serious about his life, perhaps wanting to start working with his father.

Tommy and his mother exchanged a few words, and he then asked her if she could go to the store for him because he wanted a sandwich and a coke. Shelley was glad to do it, and she initially didn't think much of it, but she began to get a very bad feeling at some point on her way to the store. As she later recalled, something about her son's behavior just didn't sit right with her.

The Ultimate Tantrum

As his funds got tighter and the prospect of being cut off from his family's money became more real, Tommy's frustration began to reach a new level. Nobody expected that Tommy would go as far as to murder his father just because he threatened to take him off the allowance. Nonetheless, Shelley remembered how she was suddenly overcome with an ominous feeling as she went on her way to the store. Halfway there, Shelley decided to turn around and head back home.

Her intuition pressed her with increasingly dark ideas as she got closer to home. Once she entered, she was immediately greeted by the sight of her husband lying on the floor, showing no signs of consciousness. Tommy was nowhere to be seen, and Shelley assumed that the two had a fight that left Thomas Sr. knocked out. As she got closer and began to examine her husband, she quickly uncovered the horrific sight of a gunshot wound in his head and a gun in his hand.

Shelley was able to get a grip on the initial shock rather quickly, and she called 911. In a composed manner, she informed the dispatcher that her husband was shot in the head and that he was most likely dead. When the dispatcher asked Shelley who shot her husband, she said that it was her son, whom she had believed to be "nuts" for a long time, but not crazy enough to kill anyone, let alone his own father.

When NYPD officers and investigators arrived, they questioned Shelley, and she revealed that she always knew her son was unstable. She explained that he had a history of mental illness, the signs of which first emerged when he was a teenager. Obsessive-compulsive disorder (OCD) and even schizophrenia were among the issues that she and some experts suspected, but Tommy was always difficult to work with, and he didn't end up receiving much help.

The police then put out an APB on Tommy, and his phone was traced only six hours after the killing. The phone's position was triangulated to his apartment in Chelsea, and the police immediately went there. When the officers arrived, Tommy didn't try to resist or run away. He simply opened the door and informed the officers that he was already talking to his lawyer on the phone. He was immediately arrested, and it didn't take the police long to bring forth charges, including that of murder and illegal possession of a firearm.

Detective Richard Tirelli and other homicide investigators began to uncover other interesting things about Tommy as the investigation went underway. They found out from his friends and acquaintances that he was at the center of an incidence of arson in 2014, where he was the main suspect, although he was never charged. The fire happened at the Hamptons home of Peter Smith Sr., whose son, Peter Smith Jr., had an altercation with Tommy after their friendship went sour. The two had even gotten into a fight on a previous occasion, leading to Smith Jr.'s broken nose but no charges being pressed.

Other discoveries, such as the Internet search history on Tommy's computer, illustrated the premeditated nature of his father's murder. Apart from the correspondence he shared with the person who sold him the gun, Tommy's attempts to hire a contract killer were particularly noteworthy. This was evident by the fact that he had searched for websites such as "Hire-a-Killer.com," "Find-a-Hitman.com," and others. This was in addition to testimonies from numerous friends who said Tommy harbored anger and aggression toward his father for some time.

According to the prosecution, the final straw was the reduction to $300, which happened on the morning of the killing. The fact that Tommy had already armed himself and researched killers-for-hire indicated the idea had been growing in his mind for a while. Detective Tirelli was of the opinion that Tommy took his gun and went to his father's house that morning to try and threaten him into paying the full allowance again. Since he didn't get what he wanted, Tirelli postulated that Tommy shot his father, "being the spoiled brat he was."

The defense focused on Tommy's mental health and tried to make the case that he was unfit to be on trial. They argued he not only had longstanding mental issues but that these problems were getting worse while he was incarcerated. Indeed, the defense was able to get multiple psychologists and mental health professionals to testify that Tommy was mentally unfit to defend himself on trial. Unfortunately for him, the prosecutors were able to get their own experts to vouch for the opposite.

Even though the outcome of the trial was perhaps not as clear-cut as the prosecution had hoped, the judge did ultimately take their side. The trial went underway despite the defense's protests, and among the witnesses was Shelley. Shelley testified that her son was unstable and not of sound mind when he killed Thomas Sr., and the defense was somewhat successful in presenting the case of Tommy's insanity. The jury eventually found him guilty of second-degree murder on top of two counts of second-degree illegal firearm possession. In autumn of 2019, Tommy was sentenced to thirty years to life in prison, with the possibility of parole in 2044. Shelley has since stood by her son, trying to get him psychiatric help while also announcing that she will appeal her son's conviction.

A Problem Child

As clear-cut and direct as Tommy's motive seemed during and after the trial, facts did come out to indicate that he had been a troubled young man for quite a while before the murder. Tommy began to exhibit issues at a young age, and initially, these didn't seem all that problematic. However, as he got older, many of his problems would get progressively worse. Unfortunately, the early warning signs were left largely ignored and, at best, poorly addressed. Tommy's parents and his teachers and professors could have perhaps done more to set Tommy straight while he was still young.

In the time since the tragedy that befell the Gilberts, Tommy's mother has been particularly outspoken and active in bringing to light what she believes are serious mental issues that her son has been struggling with his whole life. Shelley believes that the murder of Thomas Sr., like many other incidents and shortfalls of Tommy's life before that point, can be attributed to mental illness. In her estimation, the prosecution's efforts to paint Tommy as a spoiled and lazy rich kid who killed his dad out of a tantrum were unfair. Shelley has argued that her son has had a long history of mental issues, for which he never received adequate help.

As it turned out, the family's struggle with Tommy's psychotic episodes went on for some fifteen years prior to the tragedy. Shelley recalled that she was careful with her son when he was a young student attending the Deerfield Academy. She made sure that Tommy didn't overwork himself, and she did her best to help him enjoy as much of his childhood as he could. Tommy was particularly adept at mathematics, and he showed a knack for numbers from the earliest age. At Deerfield, Tommy was generally praised as a great student with a strong work ethic. He was so successful, in fact, that he got admitted to Princeton early. His advisor's report noted Tommy as having a "positive, upbeat attitude" as well as a great sense of humor and confidence.

This was when certain oddities in Tommy's behavior slowly started to emerge. The bright and confident kid that Tommy used to be gradually gave way to a new, quieter version of him. Shelley recalled that she felt he was perhaps just getting exhausted from all his hard work at school, but it was Thomas Sr. who suspected more was at play. The initial signs indicated that Tommy might have OCD, which tends to manifest through various irrational fears and all sorts of involuntary behavior. Like many others OCD sufferers, Tommy developed a severe fear of germs. He began adding more and more things to the list of "contaminated" objects that he avoided, eventually perceiving the apartment as such.

Tommy's parents tried to help him, but he was very uncooperative. It took them quite a while to get him to talk to a psychiatrist, by which time he had turned eighteen. Things were getting so bad that some of the psychiatrists recommended hospitalization to treat Tommy. Shelley later described how she was once able to read her son and get through to him "remarkably well," and how this gradually changed to a point where she felt like her own son was a stranger.

College was when things really started to deteriorate for Tommy, especially once he came into contact with drugs. Apart from marijuana, Tommy also used hallucinogens and other hard drugs, which made his mental health worse. He soon began to struggle with insomnia and would frequently withdraw to hotels, not speaking to anyone.

It wasn't long until Tommy started to have run-ins with the law as well, which illustrated the seriousness of the situation on a whole new level to his parents. At that point, the Gilberts hired a lawyer, Alex Spiro, who also had an extensive background in psychiatry, in an attempt to somehow get their son institutionalized so he could get the help he needed. However, these attempts failed as there was no legal basis to involuntarily commit him for more than 72 hours.

His conflict with Peter Smith Jr. was a particularly troubling episode. The altercation got so bad that Peter later testified that Tommy had tried to kill him. Tommy avoided an arson charge due to a lack of evidence, but there were no suspects other than him. Shelley said that this was the first time Tommy ever got violent, despite all his mental problems. She had no idea how bad things would get.

After the murder of Thomas, Alex Spiro believed that the criminal justice system should have required mental health conditions. Similarly, Shelley believes that it was the system that failed her son and is ultimately to blame for her husband's untimely death. Had the state of New York provided the help that Tommy needed, Shelley argued, her husband would probably be alive. The Gilberts did make very real attempts to have their son hospitalized. At one point, they even devised a plan to have him committed to a private mental hospital while providing a cover story to his friends that he was in Africa on a surfing trip. It was up to Tommy to sign the papers and give his consent, which he got close to doing, but he ultimately refused.

CHAPTER EIGHT:

Martin Ruddy

The murder of Eric and Carol Ruddy at the hands of their son Martin was a particularly coldblooded and perhaps unusually remorseless crime, which shocked Elswick and the Newcastle community in the North East region of England. The fact that it was motivated solely by monetary gain and that the killer was coldly calculated in the way he tried to hide and misrepresent his misdeeds would contribute to a hefty sentence. The judge described Martin's conduct after the murder of his parents as a "web of deceit."

The crime and motive's highly premeditated and materialistic nature was shocking, but so was the violence itself. For most of us, it's impossible to imagine killing our own parents just to save ourselves from financial ruin, which is why many people tried to identify some other motive that Martin might have had. In the end, it was difficult to maintain controversy after examining the facts of the case. What makes the crime even more difficult to believe is that Martin had no history of violence, and his relationship with his parents had been normal. It's hard to ascertain what might have happened in Martin's head to lead him down this road, but this is a question that even he might not be able to answer.

Hard Times

In the time leading up to the killings, Martin Ruddy, a 28-year-old father from South Tyneside, had accumulated considerable financial debts and was going through a rough time. As he later told the court, things got so difficult at one point that he went to a beach in November of 2014 with tablets and vodka, planning to take his own life. He ultimately changed his mind, but he got close, being turned back only by the fact that he had people who cared about and depended on him. Martin owed some 6,000 British pounds and was participating in a debt management problem. According to his trial testimony, he was planning to file for bankruptcy and fix his problems the legitimate way.

At the same time, Martin was aware his father had been saving a hefty retirement sum for a while, which amounted to almost 90,000 pounds. Eric planned to retire with this money and take care of Carol, who had been partially disabled ever since she suffered a stroke some nine years prior. Before the stroke, Carol worked at Newcastle

University, but the stroke left her unable to continue. In the event of Eric and Carol's deaths, Martin Ruddy stood to inherit Eric's savings as the sole beneficiary.

As the court determined, Martin saw this money as his way out, and he wanted it as soon as possible. During the trial, Martin explained how even though he was going through financial hardships, he didn't ask his father for help in late 2014. Despite his suicidal episode and his encroaching debts, it would appear that Martin determined his best course of action would be premeditated murder. This was most likely something that Martin thought about for a while before the crime, and he devised a rather diabolical plan for how he would do it and then get away with it.

In his subsequent attempts to make his burglary story seem more plausible, Martin spoke highly of his parents and only had good things to say about their relationship. Unwittingly, these testimonies only served to make his heinous crime look that much worse to everyone else. The more he tried to make it seem impossible that he killed them simply by virtue of Eric and Carol being good parents, the more disgusted he made people feel. At the same time, the fact that his parents were such decent people and that they treated him well made the case more bewildering.

People involved with the case, as well as those keeping up with the news, found it difficult to fathom why Martin would suddenly decide to go down such an extreme and dark road. The bewilderment came and still comes from the fact that Martin had other options. He could have tried to solve his financial woes in a number of ways on his own, but he could have also just asked his parents for help. According to some accounts, Martin did receive some financial assistance from his parents during his difficult period, but it wasn't enough. The program that Martin was in to try and pay the money back didn't work out. The financial problems and other tensions at home were also a significant strain on his marriage, which was close to the breaking point as Martin became more agitated in the time leading up to the killings.

It stands to reason that Martin's parents would have provided additional assistance if he had asked, but this is something that nobody will ever know to a certainty. It would seem that the prospect of getting close to 90,000 pounds right away was ultimately the most appealing to Martin. Besides, it's possible he felt that he had devised the perfect crime, so it's questionable whether he even expected to be arrested and especially convicted.

The killings on December 12 of 2014, were gruesome, to say the least. Martin first drugged his parents with anti-depressants that he had procured by lying to a psychiatrist. Martin was able to get a prescription after claiming his father had died, and he was going through a difficult time because of the loss. It hasn't been determined beyond a reasonable doubt whether he drugged his parents to make the killings easier, thus making the crime completely premeditated.

Another possibility is that he tried to make his dad more agreeable and easier to manipulate, as Martin had possibly hoped to get his dad's retirement money from him directly. Either way, Eric had no intention of giving the money to Martin, even though he was the sole beneficiary of his will. While he was alive, Eric's priority was to use the money to care for his disabled wife. Martin was supposed to get whatever remained after his parent's deaths.

At one point, things got severely physical, and Martin ended up bashing his father's head in with a brick, bludgeoning him many times. As his father was dying, Martin took a knife and started cutting his face in an attempt to make it look like Eric was attacked by a knife-wielding burglar. After that, Martin took a pair of nail scissors and stabbed himself in the chest to give additional weight to his narrative and make himself look like a victim. He also hit himself with the brick that he used to kill his dad.

The Web of Deceit

As Carol heard the commotion and stumbled upon the gruesome scene of violence, she tried to call the police. Martin rushed to stop her, and he ended up strangling his mother to death with a TV HDMI cable in the process. The emergency call, which Carol did manage to place, later ended up being a point of some controversy in regard to this case. Namely, the police received the call, but the dispatcher chose to ignore it because it was "too muffled." This call came in at 9:30, and the dispatch operator later recalled that the only intelligible part of it was, "Please hurry up."

The failure of the police dispatch to process the call and send help later caused quite a stir and led to some immediate revisions of the police procedures in regard to 999 emergency calls in England. Indeed, the operator had done nothing wrong and was just following already established procedures. The operator could neither understand what was being said nor detect any signs of distress. As per standard procedure, the operator waited an additional 45 seconds, after which the decision was made not to connect the call to the police.

There was no follow-up call for a whole hour until the police were called again from a neighbor's house, telling them that there was an attack on Eric and Carol. What had happened was that Martin, after he killed his parents and stabbed himself in the chest, ran out to his parents' next-door neighbors and told them that burglars had broken into the home and viciously attacked him and his parents. The neighbor later recalled that Martin still had the small pair of nail scissors stuck in the right side of his chest, close to the shoulder. Before the police arrived, the neighbor went into Eric and Carol's home, and he saw a horrifying scene. Eric, bludgeoned and bloodied, was lying on the floor with a pillow under his head.

The neighbor and Martin then proceeded to the living room, where Carol could be seen lying on the floor with the TV cable still around her neck. Her walking stick, a testament to her helplessness against the vicious attack, was underneath her body. The neighbor later testified that, upon seeing Carol lying face down, Martin was shocked and lay down next to her, seemingly in shock and struck with grief. He then started shaking his mother, trying to see if she would wake up. During this time, the neighbor was trying to revive Eric, who, although horribly bludgeoned and cut, was apparently still showing signs of life. Other neighbors also began arriving to investigate. Martin explained to everyone that there had been intruders who took the family hostage and murdered his parents.

Post-mortem analysis proved that Carol was strangled from behind while Eric died as a result of his wounds, primarily to his head. Examiners also looked at Martin and found his injuries from getting hit with a brick mostly superficial. However, he was also bleeding from his stab wounds, which later turned out to be self-inflicted.

According to Martin, he and his parents were sitting around and watching Coronation Street and other TV programs when intruders broke into the home and attacked them. Before that, Martin said, he and his mother went shopping in Asda. After he was arrested, charged with two counts of murder, and brought to trial, it took the jury around one hour to reject his story and find him guilty on both counts. Nonetheless, Martin maintained his supposed innocence and never confessed. He said that there was a knock on the door and that his father went to answer, at which point two male intruders forced their way in. Conveniently, the two men then knocked Martin unconscious, which left him incapacitated during the attack. After he allegedly woke up, he saw that his parents had been brutalized and that the attackers were gone.

When the police arrived, they brought along an ambulance, but there was nothing that could be done for Eric and Carol. They were pronounced dead soon thereafter. The police started questioning Martin as soon as they approached him on the scene. Martin gave the investigators some rather detailed descriptions of the two supposed assailants. The problem with his story is that his word was the only thing he had backing it up. None of the forensic and other physical evidence that the police had gathered and examined at the crime scene pointed to outside intruders, while a lot of it clearly pointed to Martin.

On top of that, CCTV footage from well-placed cameras around the Newcastle terraced house in which Martin's parents lived showed no sign of any intruders or anyone matching the descriptions given by Martin.

Martin's attempts to lie to the police and construct an elaborate false narrative would reflect terribly on him during the trial. Family friends and the many relatives who would attend the trial sessions were devastated to learn the details and facts of Martin's despicable crime. The judge made sure to emphasize the sudden and unexpected betrayal that Martin had committed against his unsuspecting, trusting parents. In light of the facts, Martin became a stranger to many of his relatives who were simply dumbfounded as to how any of this could have happened.

Epilogue

During the trial, Martin Ruddy was asked by the Newcastle Crown Court to describe the relationship he had with his parents. Despite the coldblooded and deceptive nature of his gruesome crimes, Martin maintained that he had a loving relationship with Eric and Carol. He said there was a lot of care in the family, and both he and his parents would always meet each other halfway. He described his mother as a lovely woman who was witty, sociable, well-liked, and always helpful to other people. Martin's parents had a home on Bentinck Street in Elswick, Newcastle, where he often visited them.

Martin got noticeably emotional while giving this testimony in court, especially when he talked about how much joy his parents got from their grandchildren. How much of the emotion that Martin showed during the trial was genuine remains uncertain. Since his initial defense and story about intruders quickly collapsed in the eyes of the court and jury, it's possible that he tried to supplement his lack of evidence with tears, emotional scenes, and the like.

The murderer went into quite a lot of other detail regarding the relationship with his parents. His visits to their Elswick home weren't some occasional, pre-planned thing. Martin would visit his parents a few times every week, which made it clear that their relationship was very close and that there was no estrangement. Martin even described how he and his parents would greet each other, saying that he would always hug both his mom and dad. The court also got to see things like cards that Martin would send to his parents on their birthdays and mother's day and father's day.

The judge, Paul Sloan, didn't try that hard to hide his disgust with Martin's murderous actions. He also didn't hide his happiness with the jury's decision, pointing out that he was glad that they saw through Martin's "web of deceit." Judge Sloan described Martin's crime as a gross breach of trust and power, emphasizing that his parents were not just old but also drugged with medication that caused drowsiness. Carol was already disabled since her stroke, so she was virtually helpless. Eric couldn't fare much better, being a man in his 60s. On the other hand, Martin was only 29 at the time and was a physically strong individual who worked out regularly, having worked as a bouncer in the past.

The judge also emphasized the irreparable damage Martin had caused to the rest of the family, leaving them stricken with grief. The court proceedings were painful and highly emotional for the attending relatives and friends of the well-liked couple that Eric and Carol were. The brutality of the murders was made even worse by Martin's shameless deceptions and his categorical refusal to accept responsibility for what he had done. The whole ordeal proved incredibly traumatic to many people beyond just the direct victims, and the judge felt that this further aggravated Martin's crime. Martin's desperate clinging to his clumsy, fictitious story and his refusal to confess were taken into account during sentencing. He was eventually given a life sentence in prison with no possibility of parole for the first 35 years, making him eligible in 2050.

Martin's aunt, Doreen Nichol, was one of the relatives

who expressed their shock while testifying in court. She was in disbelief the entire time and was particularly struck by the sheer viciousness of how Martin killed his parents. She said that the family was torn apart by the tragedy and that they were never going to be able to reconcile with what happened. Many people who attended the trial were also shocked by the fact that Carol had managed to call the cops and that her call was ignored, with police arriving more than an hour after the killings. In effect, the police and ambulance didn't arrive until the killer decided that he was ready for them to arrive, letting his neighbors know what happened. Relatives of Eric and Carol were the ones who started the first petition for the authorities to review their emergency call procedures urgently.

Commenting on Martin's attempts to cover his tracks, the prosecutor said that he was doubtful whether Martin felt any remorse. According to him, Martin might have been remorseful in the immediate aftermath of the act, but the prosecutor believes that his sense of self-preservation was stronger, and it eventually prevailed. As another lawyer on the case said, however, Martin would have plenty of time in prison to reflect on his crimes and feel remorse if he was still capable of it.

The police officers who led the investigation were pleased with the outcome of the trial. Andy Fairlamb, the lead investigator, said that the sentence was fair and well-deserved, especially given the fact that Martin kept lying about everything. He also expressed his hope that the trial, although it unveiled many grizzly details, would provide a degree of closure to the many people who were devastated by Eric and Carol's gruesome, untimely end at the hands of the one who should have given them protection, as Judge Sloan said.

CHAPTER NINE:

Christopher Porco

Sometimes, the perpetrator can commit a grievous crime for reasons that are apparent to everyone on the surface while, at the same time, the true underlying cause remains hidden underneath. This was perhaps the case with Christopher Porco, who axed his parents to death in their bed on November 15 of 2004. Christopher had a financial surface motive in that he had a history of stealing, but the true cause that led him to actual murder was probably psychopathy.

Putting aside the gruesome nature of his vicious attack on his parents, Peter and Joan Porco, Christopher's whole demeanor and character were rather peculiar. The young man's lack of remorse and the pathological need to lie and deceive, which had been apparent for years, were some of the reasons that led the police and other people involved with the case to believe that Porco was either a sociopath or a psychopath. The defense focused primarily on the lack of physical evidence implicating Christopher while exploring other possibilities, such as a mafia connection, but ultimately failed to convince the jury.

A Pathological Liar

Christopher's relationship with his parents and his brother, Johnathan, deteriorated for some time prior to the murders. He struggled with his studies and was a disappointment to his parents, but worse yet, he had a propensity to steal, lie, and cheat, not just his parents but everyone else as well. During the trial, many witnesses came forward to give a complete picture of Christopher's past, relationships, and character, including friends, an ex-girlfriend, and a security officer who worked at Christopher's campus.

The string of burglaries that Christopher had committed in the past was a noteworthy discovery by the investigators. These burglaries targeted Christopher's own parents, whose home he had broken into on several occasions. In July 2003, Christopher broke into his parents' home and stole their laptop, which he later sold on eBay. A few months before that, he had already stolen two other computers as well as a camera and other items.

Furthermore, Christopher was running a scam on eBay in which he swindled people out of their money without sending the goods. As it turned out later, Christopher was posing as his brother Johnathan on eBay with another account, using it to lie to customers that Christopher was dead and thus unable to deliver on what was agreed.

Christopher's relationship with his parents deteriorated in March of 2004, while he was taking a trip to England. Learning about his terrible performance at the Hudson Valley Community College, which Christopher attended in Troy, NY, Joan and Peter sent him an angry email. They severely rebuked him for his poor academic performance, expressing their disbelief at how bad his interim grade report was. This was, in fact, the third time Christopher's parents what been unpleasantly surprised with his grade report, and they threatened to cut him off this time.

In his response, which he sent a few days later, Christopher lied that it was actually the college's fault since their grade registrar was allegedly faulty. Christopher was later able to get readmitted at the University of Rochester thanks to his crafty forgeries of transcripts from the Hudson Valley Community College. However, these forgeries were not allowed as evidence for the prosecution, although they are now useful as additional information regarding Porco's history and character.

Another major source of friction between Christopher and his parents was his very questionable loans. Even more questionable was how he used these loans, such as purchasing a new car. The loans were meant to finance his tuition only. By the fall semester in 2003, Christopher already had to leave the University of Rochester due to terrible grades. He managed to get readmitted the following year, though, at this point, he once again took out a loan, this time $31,000. This money was intended for various expenses relating to the university, but Christopher secured it by forging his father's signature. This was the least of his deceptions of his parents in regard to the University of Rochester, though. Christopher lied to his parents that the university itself was paying for his tuition as well.

Peter eventually found out what his son had done, and he confronted him about it, again through email, which was two weeks before the killings. After expressing his shock, Peter told Christopher that he was going to get in touch with the bank and inform them that his signature had been forged. The next day, Peter found out about the previous loan, which was acquired with a forged signature and used to purchase a new Jeep Wrangler. In a second email, Peter expressed his disappointment yet again and told Christopher about other measures he was taking to sort this mess out with the bank. Nonetheless, he finished the email by reassuring his son that he was still loved and cared about him even though he may have disappointed his parents.

When Johnathan later testified at his brother's trial, he was notably cold toward Christopher. He made no secret that their relationship had been deteriorating for a while. It seemed that Christopher was simply a problem child and that he had a difficult time getting along with anyone, family or otherwise. The police and their investigators first postulated that Christopher might be either a sociopath or psychopath, based on the information they collected during the investigation. They felt that he lacked any semblance of conscience or remorse and that his constant deception of others was a thing of pathology.

Christopher was known to engage in other, smaller lies on a regular basis. Among students, for instance, he was known as the type of person who lied about where he came from, pretending that his family was extremely wealthy when, in fact, it was ordinary. He notably lied that his family owned numerous oceanfront homes. One of the most important testimonies about this side of Christopher's personality came from none other than Peter, who confided in Michele McKay that his son was a sociopath. Finally, perhaps the strongest voice was that of Frank Perri, a professor and psychologist. He criticized the work done by the police, particularly their interviews, saying that their approach was flawed as it failed to account for Christopher's very likely sociopathic or psychopathic personality disorder.

At the very least, Christopher was an unscrupulous

young man who cared primarily about satisfying his own needs and desires, and he had no qualms with engaging in any sort of deception to get what he wants. His nature was rather well known, but nobody anticipated that he would go as far as to hack his father to death with an ax.

The Vicious Attack and Investigation

This murder drama began to unfold on November 15 of 2004, when Peter, a court clerk of the New York State Appellate Division, failed to report to Albany. A state court officer was ordered to the Porco home at 36 Brockley Drive in Delmar to investigate why Peter didn't come in that morning. When the officer entered the premises, it didn't take long for the mystery to be solved with a rather gory discovery. Not far from the front door, Peter's bloody, chopped-up corpse lay on the floor.

The county medical examiner later confirmed that the cause of Peter's death was the devastating wounds he had sustained to his head, indicating that he had been struck with an ax multiple times. The court officer immediately called the emergency services, and the cops were soon on the scene. It was only after the police arrived that Joan Porco was also found. She was still in the bedroom, lying in a blood-soaked bed, where Christopher attacked her with the same weapon that he used on his father. Shockingly, however,

Joan was still alive, and she was soon rushed to a hospital. She sustained terrible injuries and was horribly disfigured, eventually losing her left eye and a part of her skull.

Upon further investigation, the police quickly found the murder weapon in the bedroom, a fire ax belonging to Peter. The investigators were quick to put bits of evidence together and determine that the most likely suspect was Christopher, who at the time was a student at the University of Rochester, which was located around 230 miles to the west. Within a couple of hours, the police obtained a warrant for Christopher's arrest, and they put out an APB for his apprehension. Christopher was at the university at the time when officers were processing the crime scene.

An important early clue came from Joan herself. Before she was taken to a hospital, Joan was given immediate medical care. Remarkably, she was not only alive but also lucid and capable of rudimentary communication. Christopher Bowdish, a detective of Bethlehem Police, seized the opportunity and asked her if she knew who it was that attacked her. He first asked her if it was a family member, to which Joan nodded affirmatively. The detective then asked if it was Johnathan, her older son, which Joan denied. This was merely confirmation since Johnathan was a naval officer and had a strong alibi since he was stationed far from home.

When Bowdish asked if it was Christopher, Joan nodded in confirmation. This was probably the most important clue that prompted the police to get on Christopher's trail so fast, given that there wasn't too much physical evidence pointing in his direction at that time. In a bizarre twist, however, Joan would later retract this accusation. This change came after she eventually woke up from her coma at the hospital and began saying that Christopher had nothing to do with Peter's killing.

Months later, Joan still maintained the claim of her son's innocence, reiterating it in a letter that she sent to Times Union. In this letter, she also addressed the police and the DA, urging them to leave Christopher alone and look elsewhere for the *real* killer. The conflicting accounts of Joan and Detective Bowdish greatly intensified the already high media interest in the case. It wasn't long into the drama that the media started to catch wind of the many problems that had marred the relationship between Christopher and Peter. All these revelations reflected very poorly on Christopher's case.

The way Christopher "found out" about the attack on his parents was more or less an accident. It happened when a local Times Union reporter, one Simone Sebastian, called Christopher's college roommate to ask questions about the Porcos. After hearing about this call and learning that the police had begun their investigation, Christopher went back to Delmar and was soon questioned by the investigators from the Bethlehem Police Department.

Not long after setting up the crime scene, Bethlehem Police also sent investigators to Christopher's university so they could interview members of his fraternity and his other acquaintances to try and determine where he was during the early morning of November 15, 2004. Later that month, the Albany County District Attorney, Paul Clyne, put together a grand jury that was supposed to gather testimonies from numerous witnesses in a closed session. Apart from Christopher's fraternity brothers, the grand jury also summoned other friends, an ex-girlfriend, and a campus security officer. Many of these testimonies reportedly implicated Christopher and showed that he had a weak alibi. Still, it took quite a bit more time and numerous other testimonies before Christopher was finally indicted, which happened in November of 2005.

Aftermath and Proceedings

Christopher's trial was held in Goshen, Orange County, New York. Because his mother survived, he was ultimately charged with second-degree murder for his dad's killing and attempted murder in the second-degree for the grievous bodily harm that he had inflicted on his mother. In all its

21 days, the trial garnered great levels of attention and was highly covered by the media. In fact, the trial had ended up in Orange County only because the media attention in Albany was so great that the New York State court of appeals ruled that the trial should be relocated to ensure fairness.

The presiding judge at the Orange County criminal court, Jeffrey G. Berry, introduced some restrictions to prevent another media craze from happening. For most of the trial, only still cameras were allowed with no sound or video. The judge allowed videotaping only for the summations of the defense and prosecution cases as well as the verdict. Local newspapers and TV stations were particularly devoted in their coverage, of course, leading the entire community to become heavily invested.

The case was eventually also featured in a one-hour CBS documentary as part of their 48 Hours Mystery series. The causes behind such high public interest have been the subject of some speculation during and after the case. The gruesome details of the attack, Joan's survival and subsequent advocacy for her son, and the troubling correspondence between Christopher and his parents were all factors that certainly played their part.

Indeed, Joan's devotion to her son's defense really caught the public's eye as the trial went along. She didn't just send a letter to the media either. Joan was heavily invested in the case, and she maintained Christopher's innocence for the duration of the legal proceedings. She even accompanied her son to quite a few proceedings, never missing a court session.

Needless to say, Christopher's whereabouts on November 14 and 15 of 2004 were one of the most important points of contention between the prosecution and defense during the trial. During his questioning and later testimony, Christopher explained that, on the night of November 14, he fell asleep in one of his university's dormitory lounges and didn't wake up until the morning of November 15. The Bethlehem Police investigators and the prosecution called this story into question, arguing instead that Christopher was already up in the very early hours of November 15. They postulated that he had risen early, got into his car, and had driven more than three hours back to Albany to kill his parents.

To that effect, one of the most incriminating testimonies came from a neighbor, one Marshall Gokey, who lived right next to the Porcos on Brockley Drive. According to him, in the immediate aftermath of the murder, which was before 4 a.m., he saw a yellow Wrangler parked right in the driveway of the Porco residence, plain as day for all to see. The Wrangler's presence in Albany was also corroborated by employees who worked as toll booth collectors on the New York State Thruway. The first of the collectors was

John Fallon, manning the toll booth at Exit 46, just outside Rochester. He said that a yellow Wrangler matching the description of Christopher's car had already passed through his station on the night of November 14. The second collector, Karen Russell, remembered seeing the same Jeep at her station at Exit 24 in Albany. She spotted the vehicle around 2 a.m. on November 15, notable for the high speed with which it approached.

Finally, the prosecution also presented CCTV footage from four cameras at the university, showing a yellow Wrangler leaving campus grounds around 10:30 p.m. on November 14. The same cameras showed Christopher's Jeep coming back at 8:30 in the morning of November 15. The testimonies and camera footage fit very well into the prosecution's timeline of events, with the murder occurring in the early morning hours, right around the time when Marshall Gokey saw the car at the Porco residence. These testimonies and evidence were very incriminating and greatly boosted the prosecution's case, particularly in combination with the motive that investigators were able to extract from the correspondence between Christopher and his parents. Facts and testimonies of Christopher's other misdemeanors and a deteriorating relationship with Peter also made things worse for his defense.

On the other hand, the defense lawyers focused on the

fact that the police had no clear, physical evidence tying Christopher to the attack or the crime scene, in general. The murder weapon was thoroughly examined for DNA evidence or fingerprints, but the examination produced no results. The lead defense attorney, Terence Kindlon, argued that the police had done a sloppy job. They focused too hard on Christopher right from the start, implying that they had made up their minds as to his guilt before finding any evidence to support the theory. He called into question the competence of the entire Bethlehem Police Department, in general, referring to them as a "department that chases skateboarders away from 7-11."

Instead, the defense pointed to the connection between Peter's uncle, Frank Porco, and the Bonanno crime family in NYC. Frank wasn't just connected to the family – he was allegedly a high-ranking member, or captain, of this mafia organization. Christopher's lawyers argued that the police should have investigated the possibility that Peter's murder and Joan's attack were retaliation against Frank. Coincidentally, Frank's nickname in the criminal underworld was "the Fireman" due to his history as a firefighter at the NYC Fire Department. The defense argued that the use of a fire ax could have been a message.

Ultimately, the jury disagreed, despite the other evidence presented by the prosecutor, including many testimonies, footage, and likely motive for the killing. The jury found Christopher guilty on August 10 of 2006. Between the sentences on his two charges, Christopher was given a total minimum of 50 years to life.

CHAPTER TEN:

Joel Guy Jr.

As far as parricide goes, it hardly gets more horrific than the foul deeds of Joel Michael Guy Junior. On November 26, 2016, he murdered and tried to dispose of his parents in such a brutal manner that the prosecutors referred to the whole ordeal as diabolical. The brutality was only matched by the degree of premeditation and meticulous planning that went into the murders, undoubtedly making this case stick out among the rest.

The case was marked by other bizarre details apart from the murder and Joel's attempts to hide the evidence. His request to be given the death penalty if convicted, even though he pleaded not guilty to the charges brought against him, was also a notable peculiarity. Rather than seek employment to support himself, Joel chose to massacre his own parents for their life insurance policy before they could retire and cut him off his allowance.

The killings came despite the fact that his parents had supported him his entire life and continued to do so in the time leading up to their death, even though Joel Guy Jr. was in his late 20s. Joel's parents had certainly left this life in one of the worst possible ways – at the hands of a child they brought up and unconditionally supported his entire life. In many ways, Joel was and continues to be every parent's worst nightmare.

Background and Motive

Joel Michael Guy Sr. was a reputable and accomplished man who worked as a pipeline engineer, while his wife, Lisa Guy, also had a prosperous corporate career as an administrator at Jacobs Engineering in Oak Ridge, Tennessee. According to a testimony by one of Joel Jr.'s sisters during the subsequent trial, Lisa Guy spent most of her married years at home. Her career was something she started solely so she could give most of her paycheck to her son, Joel.

As can be seen, Joel Jr.'s parents were hard-working, decent people who did their best to provide for their family and weren't the type of people to get into problems with others. Joel Sr. was born in Surgoinsville, Hawkins County, Tennessee, and he had three daughters from a previous marriage. Before he was killed, he was planning to retire from his engineering job and move to Surgoinsville.

Joel Jr., on the other hand, was always somewhat peculiar. During the subsequent trial, various acquaintances and relatives testified that Joel was generally reclusive and preferred to stay shut in his room, avoiding contact even with family members. Numerous relatives said they didn't even know him well because of this lack of contact. Joel was born in 1988, and he graduated from the Louisiana School for Math, Science, and the Arts in 2006, after also having gone to Hahnville High School.

Joel also enrolled in college at one point, being admitted into George Washington University, where he only spent one semester. After that, Joel also went to Louisiana State University while living in Baton Rouge. He was planning to become a plastic surgeon, but he gradually neglected his studies, and his academic career didn't go anywhere. Joel stayed living in Baton Rouge right up to killing his parents in 2016, some ten years in total. Apart from these attempts to study and train for a profession, Joel had no history of employment and was always fully supported by his parents. Joel Jr. lived in quite a few places during his life, including Surgoinsville, Knoxville, Greensville, South Carolina, Baton Rouge, and St. Charles County in Louisiana.

During the years he spent in Baton Rouge, Joel Jr. was on his own, even though his parents financially supported him. For around a decade, he maintained this lifestyle on the basis of being a college student, although he underperformed and wasn't particularly committed to graduating. The lifestyle also played very well into Joel Jr.'s reclusive nature, allowing him to stay away from the rest of his family and everyone else for that matter. There was a record of Joel Jr. as a registered Democrat voter in Louisiana dating back to 2008.

After he left for Baton Rouge, Joel's parents kept many of his childhood toys and other belongings in his former room in the home on Goldenview Lane in Knoxville. These items were later looked at by investigators, and they included many memories, including pictures of Joel Jr. when he was a small boy.

Joel Jr. was the only child of Joel Sr. and Lisa, and there were never any indications that his parents did him wrong. According to the testimonies of his three half-sisters, their parents were fair, and Joel Sr. showed equal love, affection, and support to all of his children. According to them, it was Joel Jr. who lacked affection for his family, preferring to keep his distance and live as far away from everyone else as possible. Joel Jr. wasn't even interested in keeping in touch while he was away. His sisters and other family members had group chats where they frequently communicated, sharing jokes, personal updates, and the like. Joel Jr. never participated in such groups. One of his sisters even went as far as to testify that Joel Jr. probably didn't even know her kids' names.

Joel Jr. was ultimately a fairly disturbed individual, but his motive was very clear since his handwritten journal, referred to in the trial as a "book of premeditation," left very little room for speculation. Rather than accept the new reality and try to look for a job to support himself after this parents retired, Joel Jr.'s idea of becoming financially independent was to slaughter his parents and claim their life insurance, which he expected to be a hefty sum of around half a million USD.

In fact, the reason he chose to murder both of his parents was so he could maximize his expected payout since neither of the parents would be alive to benefit from the other's insurance. Even after the murders, while the trial was underway with him as the sole suspect, Joel Jr. would maintain his innocence and still file claims, trying to get the insurance payout he believed was coming to him.

While the direct motive was clear and more than enough for the prosecution, the true underlying problem within Joel Jr.'s head will perhaps forever be a mystery. He was found to be sane and perfectly fit to stand trial, and the degree to which he meticulously planned his crime showed he wasn't intellectually impaired. How this young man got to a point where he thought that massacring his parents for their life insurance was a legitimate course would certainly forever boggle the mind of normal people.

A Diabolical Stew of Human Remains

Things took a murderous turn when Joel Sr. and Lisa decided that enough was enough, announcing their plans to cut their son off because it was "time for Joel Michael to stand on his own feet." This decision came in the light of the couple's plans to retire and move back to Joel Sr.'s hometown. One of the testimonies that the parents had been planning to cut their son off from the allowance came from Angela Crane, one of his half-sisters. She also said that the matter of Joel Jr.'s financial independence had been a hot issue in the family for quite a while before that point.

The Guy family had already sold their house in Knoxville, located at 11434 Goldenview Lane, and things were set for their retirement in Surgoinsville. In the days leading up to the killings, the entire family, including Joel Jr. and his three half-sisters, was to come together for one last family gathering at the Knoxville house for Thanksgiving on November 24 of 2016. His sisters testified that Joel Jr. was unusually cheerful, outgoing, and seemingly happy during their Thanksgiving dinner. They all knew him to be a recluse who didn't particularly enjoy anyone's company. In fact, he even seemed to enjoy hanging out and playing with some of the children that his sister had brought over for Thanksgiving.

Joel's terrible journal and other evidence later showed

that he had been planning his crime for some time prior to this family gathering. On one of the journal's pages, there are many tips that he wrote down for himself regarding how and when to do certain things. Another notable feature of the journal is the shopping list of things that he needed for the murder and subsequent disposal of his parents' corpses. Included were things like "killing knives," "carving knives (to make small pieces)," a sledgehammer ("to crush bones"), plastic bins "for the denaturation process," lye, acid, and a range of other items.

"Get bleach – denature proteins" and "Bring blender and food grinder – grind meat" were also some of the bulletins on his horrific list, ever so casually compiled. Details on how to sanitize the entire crime scene, flush chunks of his parents down the toilet, purchase items without arousing suspicion, scrub any DNA from the premises and himself, and many other tips could be found in the journal well. In all, the grizzly meticulousness of Joel Jr.'s premeditated crime would leave those attending the subsequent trial simply stunned.

The killings began when, on November 26, Joel Jr. first attacked his father on the second floor of the house in an exercise room, stabbing him with a knife many times. At this time, Lisa was out shopping. Investigators saw clear signs of a struggle at the murder scene, with many objects turned over, broken and smashed. An autopsy on what was left of Joel Guy Sr. later found that he had sustained some 42 stab wounds or sharp force injuries, to be exact. The stabbing was so barbaric that some of Joel Sr.'s ribs were scratched while others were severed. The stabbing wreaked havoc on the man's lungs, liver, kidneys, and other organs while a piece of the murder weapon was even lodged in his shoulder muscles.

After the killing, Joel Jr. cut off his father's hands at the wrists, his arms at the shoulder blades, his legs at the hips, and also his right foot at the ankle. According to Leslie Nassios, the Knox County Assistant District Attorney, the scene in the exercise room showed that the dismembered man had fought hard for his life.

When Lisa Guy came back home from Wal-Mart, her son attacked her in the same manner he did his father, stabbing her 31 times, with 21 of those being extremely deep and severe injuries. Much like her husband, Lisa's ribs were shattered from the force of the stabbing. Joel Jr. then cut off his mother's legs below the knees and her arms at the shoulders. Joel then decapitated his mother's already-mangled corpse partly by cutting and partly by applying blunt force to break the head off the spine. He then put the head in a pot, leaving it to boil on the stove downstairs. The severed limbs that Joel had collected were placed in large containers and submerged in corrosive liquid in an attempt to dissolve them. He did the same thing with what remained of his parents' torsos.

During the struggle with his father upstairs, Joel Jr. sustained some injuries, notably a deep cut on his thumb. Surveillance cameras picked him up at the local Wal-Mart, buying bandages and other first-aid provisions to try and treat his wounds. After presumably failing to take care of his injuries, Joel Jr. decided to head back to Baton Rouge on Sunday, November 27, to have his cuts treated at his student clinic.

Back at the house, limbs and horrifically mutilated torsos were dissolving in plastic bins and containers. Lisa's head was in a pot on the stove, hands and other body parts littered the floors, and bloody clothes were in piles. Blood and tissue littered the home. Before leaving, Joel turned the heat in the house up to 90° F (32° C), hoping to make the decomposition and dissolving processes faster while he was gone. Not content with having to wait for the insurance money that he was expecting, Joel Jr. also emptied his parents' bank accounts after killing them.

Investigation, Trial, and Testimonies

In the time after Joel Jr. went back to Baton Rouge, with the nightmarish crime scene at the Guy residence not even remotely cleaned up, Lisa's boss, Jennifer Whited, started to grow suspicious over Lisa's absence. She soon called the cops, asking them to go and check on the Guy family on November 28 of 2016. The responder was a Knox County Sheriff's Office deputy, who turned up to the family residence only to find the house locked up and seemingly empty.

Additional deputies came sometime after that in a second visit, finding no answer yet again. A local realtor tipped the deputies off about a possible entrance through the garage door, which the deputies did, finally gaining access to the house. As soon as the officers entered the garage, they could already detect a nauseating smell coming from elsewhere in the house. The first discoveries that the officers made included guns, severed hands, and blood everywhere. They also found the family dog barking in frustration as he had been locked in one of the upstairs rooms. The deputies didn't want to disturb the obvious crime scene further, so they went back to report their findings.

Soon thereafter, the forensics unit arrived, along with a hazmat team in full protective, biohazard equipment to remove all the toxic, corrosive fluids. The sheer amount of evidence and just the general mess of this hellish crime scene required extensive forensic work, keeping investigators on the scene all night and for some time the next day. Joel Jr. actually returned to the house on the night of November

28, hoping to pick up where he left off, but he could see that the crime scene was set up, so he just kept on driving back to Baton Rouge. It didn't take long for the police, with the help of the FBI, to connect the dots, track Joel down, and place him under arrest on November 29.

Tracking Joel down and connecting him to the crime scene was made easier by numerous surveillance videos that he was caught on while making the rounds before and after the crime. He was recorded multiple times throughout November as he visited various stores, purchasing all the tools and products he needed for his plan. This was in addition to the recording that he was caught on while buying medical supplies after the murder.

The trial was given plenty of media attention due to the killer's almost unbelievable selfishness and brutality. It was also an incredibly emotional affair, with many testimonies given to the prosecution. Particularly striking were the victim impact testimonies, in which friends and especially family members talked about what Joel Sr. and Lisa were like and how the killings had absolutely ravaged the lives of everyone in the family from both of Joel's marriages.

Another one of Joel Jr.'s half-sisters, Chandise Fink, left quite an impression in the courtroom when she spoke directly to the jury, expressing her sorrow that they too had to let the evil of this murder case seep into their lives. She spoke of how happy, caring, cheerful, and loving Joel Sr. and Lisa were. Most importantly, she emphasized just how much they both loved Joel Jr.

The presiding Judge Steve Sword referred to Joel Jr.'s crime as "pure evil overkill," and perhaps rightly so. From his sisters to their children to family friends and other relatives, the courtroom echoed with grief-stricken weeping and many shaking testimonies as to what this monstrous crime had done to an otherwise normal, loving family.

Joel Michael Guy Jr. was eventually charged with two counts of first-degree murder, two counts of felony murder, and even two counts of abuse of a corpse. After the jury found him guilty, the court made sure that he would never leave prison. This was despite's Joel's hopes to be sentenced to death if he was found guilty. Right from the start, he pled not guilty, and he would never admit to what he had done. The defense lawyers had little evidence to support their client's innocence and instead focused on calling the prosecution's evidence into question. They did manage to get some of the evidence thrown out, particularly those bits that the police found while conducting a search of Joel's apartment, which was later determined to have been unconstitutional. The trial took only four days.

In the end, the defense could do little more than argue against giving Joel consecutive life sentences and the additional four years for the corpse abuse. They based these arguments on his lack of prior criminal history, and they also stressed that he would be an old man by the time he got out of prison, thus posing no threat. There was a minimum of 51 years that Joel could serve before being eligible for parole, but Judge Sword was unconvinced. He said that he saw no potential for rehabilitation whatsoever and that Joel Jr.'s mind was deeply troubling and unlikely to change. The judge's argument was undoubtedly bolstered by Joel Jr.'s lack of remorse or any other emotion whatsoever during the trial.

Conclusion

Both as individuals and as a society, we have a natural inclination to protect children and keep them away from all sorts of harm. We rightfully see them as vulnerable and in need of our protection. This is why it always comes as such a shock when children are the ones who are doing the harm. These cases can be very difficult to prosecute because of biases, and public pressure can often get immense.

Nonetheless, children have proven time and time again that they are capable of murder for any reason, just like adults. Parricide and other murderous incidents involving kids are also very interesting as a part of the age-old discussion on the effects of nature vs. nurture. While it's often difficult to hold children entirely accountable for such extreme incidents, the wide range of motives and circumstances we've seen implies that nature and nurture work in unison to create them when it comes to killers.

The fact that children are not fully developed individuals and aren't fully in control of themselves doesn't serve the essentialist argument. Children who kill - even when they murder their own parents in cold blood - will always have the capacity to change. In fact, nature almost guarantees that they'll change. The only question is what that change will look like.

Unfortunately, once these children end up in the correctional system, whether as juveniles or adults, their path will often lead only toward additional disasters. Children who end up in these institutions for much lesser crimes will often live a life of crime, let alone those who find themselves the main actors in a real-life murder drama. Perhaps it's asking too much of society to sympathize with killers, but if anyone has hope of salvaging what's left of their lives after these grueling tragedies, it's the children, guilty or not. To that end, juveniles are undoubtedly the one group of offenders where we can agree that rehabilitation should always take precedence over punishment. However, not all children are juveniles, and in those cases, one person's child is another's monster.

References

A Parent's Murder and a 16-Year-old Daughter's Conviction: The Sarah Johnson Parricide Case. (2018, June 17). Crime Traveller. https://www.crimetraveller.org/2018/06/sarah-johnson-parricide-case/

Alex And Derek King Teen Killers | My Crime Library. (2021). Mycrimelibrary.com. https://mycrimelibrary.com/alex-and-derek-king-teen-killers/

All That's Interesting. (2018, May 21). *Jasmine Richardson Killed Her Family With Her "Werewolf" Boyfriend — Now She's Walking Free.* All That's Interesting; All That's Interesting. https://allthatsinteresting.com/jasmine-richardson

BISHOP, L. (2019, November 15). *Christopher Porco case recalled 15 years later.* WRGB. https://cbs6albany.com/news/local/christopher-porco-delmar-murder-15-years-later

Bonvillian, C., & Desk, C. M. G. N. C. (n.d.). *Life in prison: Joel Guy Jr. convicted of brutal 2016 murders, dismemberment of parents.* KIRO 7 News Seattle. Retrieved from https://www.kiro7.com/news/trending/joel-guy-jr-convicted-brutal-2016-murders-dismemberment-parents-sentenced-life/

Canedy, D. (2002, November 15). Florida Boys Admit They Killed Father; Shorter Term Is Set. *The New York Times.* https://www.nytimes.com/2002/11/15/us/florida-boys-admit-they-killed-father-shorter-term-is-set.html

Canedy, D. (2003, March 6). Man Guilty Of Concealing Boys' Killing Of

Father. *The New York Times.* https://www.nytimes.com/2003/03/06/us/man-guilty-of-concealing-boys-killing-of-father.html

Cooperman, J. (2011, June 21). *A Conversation With Stacey Lannert.* Www. stlmag.com. https://www.stlmag.com/A-Conversation-With-Stacey-Lannert/

Crocker, B. (n.d.). *Joel Guy Jr. gets two life sentences - one after the other - in parents' murders.* Knoxville News Sentinel. Retrieved from https://www.knoxnews.com/story/news/crime/2020/11/19/joel-guy-jr-two-life-sentences-killing-parents-tennessee/3764870001/

Deathwish, G. (2020, October 11). *A "Very, Very, Rare Crime": The Guy Murders (True Crime).* Horrorfuel.com. http://horrorfuel.com/2020/10/11/a-very-very-rare-crime-the-guy-murders-true-crime/

DelhiMay 27, I. T. W. D. N., May 28, 2016UPDATED:, & Ist, 2016 16:20. (n.d.). *Head smashed with an axe, but not dead yet: When a man did his daily chores until his last breath.* India Today. Retrieved from https://www.indiatoday.in/fyi/story/man-did-his-daily-chores-until-his-last-breath-porco-case-man-died-325962-2016-05-27

Desk, C. B., Cox Media Group National Content. (n.d.). *"Diabolical stew of human remains": Graphic details mark start of man's trial in parents' 2016 murders.* WFXT. https://www.boston25news.com/news/trending/diabolical-stew-human-remains-graphic-details-highlight-start-mans-trial-parents-murders/

Eric and Carol Ruddy murders: Family call for 999 changes. (2015, July 20). *BBC News.* https://www.bbc.com/news/uk-england-tyne-33600777

Eric and Carol Ruddy murders: Son "staged burglary." (2015, June 8). *BBC News.* https://www.bbc.com/news/uk-england-tyne-33048826

Esmie Tseng | Murderpedia, the encyclopedia of murderers. (n.d.). Murderpedia. org. https://murderpedia.org/female.T/t/tseng-esmie.htm

From Abuse Victim to Killer to Public Defender - Stacey Lannert • Morbidology. (2020, February 14). Morbidology. https://morbidology.com/from-abuse-victim-to-killer-to-public-defender-stacey-lannert/

Gavin, R. (2021a, March 15). *Law Beat: The endless legal battle of "Romeo Killer: The Chris Porco Story."* Times Union. https://www.timesunion.com/news/article/Law-Beat-The-endless-legal-battle-of-Romeo-16021647.php

Gavin, R. (2021b, March 17). *Chris Porco takes legal battle versus Lifetime to appeals court.* Times Union. https://www.timesunion.com/news/article/Chris-Porco-takes-legal-battle-versus-Lifetime-to-16032970.php

Harris, A. (n.d.). *Knox Co. parents found dissolving in "diabolical stew of human remains," investigators say.* Https://Www.wvlt.tv. Retrieved from https://www.wvlt.tv/2020/09/28/live-opening-statements-begin-in-trial-for-man-accused-of-dismembering-parents-at-knox-co-home/

History.com Editors. (2009, November 13). *The Menendez brothers murder their parents.* HISTORY. https://www.history.com/this-day-in-history/the-menendez-brothers-murder-their-parents

Is Esmie Evil? (2006, January 5). The Pitch. https://www.thepitchkc.com/is-esmie-evil/

"I've waited a long time for this" || Joel Guy Jr. guilty of murdering, dismembering parents in 2016. (n.d.). Wbir.com. Retrieved from https://www.wbir.com/article/news/crime/joel-guy-jr-guilty-of-murdering-and-dismembering-parents-in-2016/51-7498ca31-6088-4fe4-86f2-9636e236d925

Jasmine Richardson. (n.d.). Deadly Women Wiki. Retrieved from https://deadlywomen.fandom.com/wiki/Jasmine_Richardson

Juan Ignacio Blanco. (2019). *Christopher Porco | Murderpedia, the encyclopedia of murderers.* Murderpedia.org. https://murderpedia.org/male.P/p/porco-christopher.htm

Judge allows use of some evidence in dismemberment murder case; other requests

pending. (n.d.). Wbir.com. Retrieved from https://www.wbir.com/article/news/crime/parental-dismemberment-son-due-in-court-friday-in-parents-murders/51-e8e2017c-2745-4e98-a58a-f5095bf368b7

Kennedy, R. (2015a, June 18). *Man accused of murdering parents pays tribute to "lovely mam."* Mirror. https://www.irishmirror.ie/news/world-news/martin-ruddy-man-accused-murdering-5902573

Kennedy, R. (2015b, June 26). *Double murderer Martin Ruddy must serve at least 35 years behind bars.* ChronicleLive. https://www.chroniclelive.co.uk/news/north-east-news/double-murderer-martin-ruddy-must-9532515

Kennedy, R. (2015c, June 26). *Ex bouncer who drugged and murdered parents jailed for 35 years.* Mirror. https://www.mirror.co.uk/news/uk-news/martin-ruddy-ex-bouncer-who-5952426

Killer daughter case ignites US debate. (2006, May 3). *News.bbc.co.uk.* http://news.bbc.co.uk/2/hi/americas/4967340.stm

lml01. (2012, November 30). *She Suffered, Shattered, Shot, and Served Time.* Killers without Conscience. https://krazykillers.wordpress.com/2012/11/30/she-suffered-shot-and-served-time/

Lyle & Erik Menendez | Murderpedia, the encyclopedia of murderers. (n.d.). Murderpedia.org. Retrieved from https://murderpedia.org/male.M/m/menendez-brothers.htm

Martin Ruddy convicted of killing parents in Newcastle home. (2015, June 25). *BBC News.* https://www.bbc.com/news/uk-england-tyne-33266358

Martin Ruddy jailed for 35 years for killing parents. (2015, June 26). *BBC News.* https://www.bbc.com/news/uk-england-tyne-33286051#:~:text=A%20man%20who%20bludgeoned%20his

Menza, K. (2017, September 26). *The Menendez Murders.* Town & Country; Town & Country. https://www.townandcountrymag.com/society/money-and-power/a12231370/menendez-brothers-murders-trial-why-they-did-it-story/

Monacelli, A. (n.d.). *Jasmine Richardson, Jeremy Steinke, and the Richardson Family Murders.* Soapboxie. Retrieved from https://soapboxie.com/government/Murderous-Children-Jasmine-Richardson#gid=ci02 73868ef00027eb&pid=murderous-children-jasmine-richardson-MTc1MTI4MTM1NDU1NTQ5MjUy

News, A. B. C. (n.d.-a). *"Entitled" son gets max sentence for killing his father for reducing his allowance.* ABC News. Retrieved from https://abcnews.go.com/US/entitled-son-max-sentence-killing-father-reducing-allowance/story?id=65902157

News, A. B. C. (n.d.-b). *King Brothers' Mom On Boys' Guilty Pleas.* ABC News. Retrieved from https://abcnews.go.com/GMA/story?id=125599&page=1

News, A. B. C. (n.d.-c). *Primetime Crime: Teen Charged With Parents' Gruesome Murder.* ABC News. Retrieved from https://abcnews.go.com/TheLaw/story?id=3451371&page=1&singlePage=true#.TrLDGfQr2so

Perry, J. (2021, March 22). *How Forbidden Love Drove 12-year-old Jasmine Richardson To Murder Her Family.* Talk Murder to Me. https://talkmurder.com/jasmine-richardson/

Pleasance, C. (2015, June 26). *Broke son who murdered his parents for money given two life sentences.* Mail Online. https://www.dailymail.co.uk/news/article-3140807/Debt-ridden-former-doorman-murdered-parents-money-staged-break-cover-tracks-given-two-life-sentences.html

Rosenberg, R., & Saul, E. (2019, September 27). *Ivy League killer Thomas Gilbert Jr. gets 30 years to life in shooting death of millionaire dad.* New York Post. https://nypost.com/2019/09/27/ivy-league-killer-thomas-gilbert-jr-gets-30-years-to-life-prison-sentence/

RR, A. (n.d.). *Sarah Marie Johnson.* Forensic Files Now. Retrieved from https://forensicfilesnow.com/index.php/tag/sarah-marie-johnson/

Sadler, M. (n.d.). *Who is Joel Guy Jr.?* Https://Www.wvlt.tv. https://www.wvlt. tv/2020/09/29/who-is-joel-guy-jr/

Sandoval, E. (2019, September 27). Princeton Graduate Killed Father Over Allowance. He Got 30 Years to Life. *The New York Times.* https://www. nytimes.com/2019/09/27/nyregion/thomas-gilbert-murder-sentence. html

Sarah Johnson | Murderpedia, the encyclopedia of murderers. (n.d.). Murderpedia. org. Retrieved from https://murderpedia.org/female.J/j/johnson-sarah. htm

Stacey Lannert | Murderpedia, the encyclopedia of murderers. (n.d.). Murderpedia. org. https://murderpedia.org/female.L/l/lannert-stacey.htm

Staveley, J. (2019, April 8). *When she was 12, Jasmine Richardson planned the murder of her family. Now she's walking free.* Mamamia. https://www. mamamia.com.au/jasmine-richardson/

Sutton, C. (2016, August 18). *Ten years after "werewolf" massacre of her family girl walks free.* NewsComAu; news.com.au. https://www.news.com.au/ lifestyle/real-life/news-life/jasmine-richardson-walks-free-a-decade-after-as-a-12yearold-she-and-werewolf-boyfriend-massacred-her-family/news-story/f826a2b4efb359bd02b53c4066234bae

The Porco murder: Did a college student take an ax to his parents? (n.d.). Www. cbsnews.com. Retrieved from https://www.cbsnews.com/news/the-porco-murder-did-a-college-student-take-an-ax-to-his-parents/

Tyneside man convicted of killing his parents. (n.d.). ITV News. Retrieved from https://www.itv.com/news/tyne-tees/story/2015-06-25/tyneside-man-convicted-of-killing-his-parents/

Vecsey, T. (2020a, January 16). *Son Gets 30 Years, Mother Speaks Out.* The East Hampton Star. https://www.easthamptonstar.com/police-courts/2020116/son-gets-30-years-mother-speaks

Vecsey, T. (2020b, January 23). *Tommy Gilbert's Agonizing Descent*. The East Hampton Star. https://www.easthamptonstar.com/police-courts/2020123/tommy-gilberts-agonizing-descent

Vecsey, T. (2020c, January 30). *Storm Signals Flew Before a Murder*. The East Hampton Star. https://www.easthamptonstar.com/police-courts/2020130/storm-signals-flew-murder

Why Did Ivy League Hedge Fund Heir Thomas Gilbert Jr. Murder His Father? (2020, August 10). Oxygen Official Site. https://www.oxygen.com/snapped/crime-news/why-thomas-gilbert-jr-ivy-league-dad-killer-murder-father

Williams, A. (2015, July 1). *Police fail to respond to murder call because voice was "too muffled."* Mail Online. https://www.dailymail.co.uk/news/article-3145565/Grandmother-s-desperate-999-call-husband-murdered-son-NOT-passed-police.html

Witnesses describe graphic scene at Porco home. (2006, June 29). Times Union. https://www.timesunion.com/news/article/Witnesses-describe-graphic-scene-at-Porco-home-580222.php

Worthen, M. (2017, September 25). *Everything You Wanted to Know About the Menendez Brothers Case*. Biography. https://www.biography.com/news/menendez-brothers-murder-case-facts

Made in the USA
Coppell, TX
26 June 2022

79294734R00089